Meet Sri Paul Twitchell—

the most amazing spiritual leader known today . . .

—A shy American who, shunning publicity, has led millions on a new pathway to God . . .

—A healer who has rescued as many from physical ills and mental anguish . . .

—The teacher of a unique secret science as old as Time and as new as Tomorrow . . .

The wisdom and deeds of this modern wonder-worker are bringing increasingly new light—and hope—to a troubled world.

YOU OWE IT TO YOURSELF TO READ HIS STORY—NOW!

IN MY SOUL
I AM FREE

By Brad Steiger

The internationally bestselling story of America's own

PAUL TWITCHELL

—prophet, healer, soul-traveler—whose miraculous cures
may even now be helping you!

IN MY SOUL I AM FREE
The Incredible Paul Twitchell Story

For a free catalogue of other books printed by
Illuminated Way Press please write:

Illuminated Way Press
P.O. Box 82388
San Diego, CA 92138

CONTENTS

PART I

PART II

Foreword

I have written many books since I authored IN MY SOUL I AM FREE, the Paul Twitchell story, in 1968. I have related well-documented accounts of many extraordinary men and women. I have explored the possibilities of haunted houses, unidentified flying objects, precognition, ancient civilizations, and the contemporary revelatory experience. I have talked with seers, shamans, and a wide variety of psychic superstars. Interestingly enough, regardless of my lecture topic, regardless of the material which I am discussing over radio or television talk shows, the question and answer period or the call-in portion of the show inevitably brings in queries about Paul Twitchell. In the five years since I wrote IN MY SOUL, I doubt strongly if I have ever done a single personal appearance during which at least one person did not ask me for my impressions of Paul and the Eckankar movement.

Paul telephoned me just a few days before his death. It was a strange kind of call, and I pondered the reason for it. There had been a time when Paul would telephone me, and we would engage in a leisurely kind of conversation about nothing in particular. That had been an earlier time, a time before I became an author in demand and Paul became the Living Eck Master, the spiritual leader of thousands. This call was that kind of unhurried, non-specific conversation, a return to a pattern we had come to break because of the increased obligations of our heavy workloads. I cradled the receiver wondering why Paul had called. Within a week, the reason became clear to me. Paul had telephoned me to say *au revoir*.

For this special edition of IN MY SOUL I AM FREE, I have prepared a transcript of the taped speech which I sent to the 1971 World Wide Seminar in Las Vegas when Darwin Gross received the rod of Eck power and became the new living Eck master. My speech was in the nature of a personal memorial to Paul Twitchell, who had left the earth plane a little more than a month before the annual gathering of Eckists. Herewith are my remembrances of Paul Twitchell:

My association with Paul Twitchell began when I included a chapter on him in my book, THE ENIGMA OF REINCARNATION (Ace Books, 1967). The mail response to that single chapter was enormous, to say the least.

I included a chapter on Paul in a second book entitled BEYOND UNSEEN BOUNDARIES, which was published by Popular Library. The mail response to that one chapter was so heavy that the publisher, the editor, the mailroom, wondered what was going on. They were receiving upwards of 50 to 100 letters a day. Now, this is all the more remarkable because Popular Library does not give its full address in its books, but simply, Popular Library, New York, N.Y.

I was contacted shortly thereafter by the editor, through my agent, who asked if I would prepare a biography of Paul Twitchell, due to the enormous mail response which had been received. I said I would certainly attempt to do this, but I did not know if Mr. Twitchell would consent to a biography at that time.

I contacted Paul, and he said that he would consider it. After a few days, he called and said, yes, he would approve of me as his official biographer; and he would be happy to have a book done about him. At that time or perhaps in the interim, the publisher had seen my outline, and since he happened to be a very strong orthodox Christian, he said absolutely no way would Popular Library do the Paul Twitchell story.

There I was. I had a verbal agreement from Paul. I had done a brief outline. Now what was I to do? Give it up?

Well, I thought if there was that great an excitement, that great a response, which could be prompted by a single chapter in two books, this must be a man who was saying something of great importance to a great many people. I took the project back to my agent, who in turn took it to Lancer Books, who said at once, yes, let's do it, but we need a letter of permission to Brad from Paul Twitchell.

Paul had left for a seminar in Dallas, Texas, I believe, at that time. He was out of touch, but I managed to contact Gail, and she said that she would telephone Paul and he would call me. Within a few hours Paul himself was telling me that he was pleased with what was happening and that he would send me a letter of permission.

I must emphasize that my agent had kept repeating to me that the entire deal was contingent upon Paul giving his permission and doing so in writing. When I told him that I did not know if I could produce such a document within a few days because Paul would be incommunicado, my agent became very upset. He became very concerned that the deal was going to fall through.

When Paul contacted me and said that a letter would be coming, I called my agent the next morning to relieve his anxiety. He was not anxious when I talked to him, however, because he said: "You know, it's the funniest thing. As I was waking up in my beach house this morning, there appeared at the foot of my bed the figure of a man, a rather tall man, who seemed to look like a monk or a priest or at least had a cowl over his head, and then the image seemed to swirl away to that of a smaller man, a smaller man who spoke with kind of a southern accent, but in a way a more precise manner of speaking, almost

English. This man said to me, 'Don't worry, I've given Brad permission.' "Now," he said, "wasn't that a funny dream?"

At the time, I, too, thought it had been a funny dream, but I was struck by my agent's description of the accent with which the illusion-hallucination-dream spoke as being suspiciously similar to the manner in which Paul Twitchell spoke.

The book which you know as IN MY SOUL I AM FREE was originally entitled, THE WIND FROM HEAVEN. This was the title that Paul liked and which I had sent in as the title for the biography of Paul Twitchell. The book, IN MY SOUL I AM FREE, was released just before Paul was leaving for Europe. I must tell you that he was quite concerned and more than a little upset that the title of the book had been changed to a title that he did not like at all. Paul was really very agitated about this, but he said, "I'm not going to trouble myself anymore. I'm just getting ready to go to Europe and Gail is going with me, but we'll talk about this when I get back and then we'll see what we can do about this."

I said, "Well, they're not going to change the title. They're not going to redo the cover."

Paul mumbled a little bit and with just a touch of a growl to his voice said, "Okay, we'll talk when I get back from Europe."

Paul and Gail went to Europe; I went on a promotion and publicity tour; and I do not know which of us worked the harder. Publicity tours are not as glamorous as they might be portrayed. They are really a great deal of difficult and emotionally taxing work. A promotion tour is hitting one city after another and spending a lot of nights in lonely hotel rooms. But, at any rate, as you well know, the book IN MY SOUL I AM FREE became a great success, went into several different editions, and sold several hundred thousand copies, so that by the time

Paul got back from Europe, he was not too concerned anymore that WIND FROM HEAVEN had blown into IN MY SOUL I AM FREE.

It is difficult to try to select what things to share with you. Paul and I had many fine times together. There were many nights when we talked until dawn. We always had a stimulating exchange of ideas. I suppose there are many things that I know about him that not many others know — some of his thoughts, ideas, plans, and aspirations. He outlined — it is difficult for me to learn to speak of Paul in the past tense — many plans for the future of ECKANKAR which I hope someday soon will be realized. Perhaps there are those among you now who will carry through the ideas, the projects, which Paul Twitchell visualized as being the physical embodiment, action, and strength of ECKANKAR.

I think of one demonstration of Paul's unique abilities which I suppose I shall never forget. My wife and I received a call from Paul, saying that he was flying back from a seminar — it seems like it had been in Cleveland — and that he would be staying over in Minneapolis. He invited us to drive up to the hotel — rooms and meals on him. Paul was very fond of doing this kind of thing, of giving us a call and saying, let's get together. He always prepared a very fine table, with the help of the chefs at the hotels at which he stayed. He was a good host away from home. On this particular occasion, he had invited my secretary (who has now become a writer in her own right, Jeanyne), my wife, and myself to come to Minneapolis to talk and have some relaxation.

We had about a three-hour drive to Minneapolis and the airport. Our car had been in perfect working order, but as we were pulling away from the airport after having met Paul, we noticed that neither of the turn signals worked. My wife Marilyn became very concerned about driving in heavy traffic without our blinker lights, because we could not signal when we changed from one lane to another. She was getting very worried about our getting picked up or incurring the chagrin of motorists behind us and in front of us. Finally in desperation she said, "Well, Paul, *heal* the turn signals!"

I felt very embarrassed for my wife's agitation, and I said, "Honey, Paul works with people, not with automobiles." But Paul said, "No, that's all right. Maybe for cars it takes longer, but that's all right."

We laughed a bit, thinking that Paul had turned my wife's agitation into a subject for jest to relieve the tension. Then we saw a gas station up ahead and since the signal lights did not work — I was pushing with all my might one way or the other way, jiggling them, banging them; they absolutely didn't work — I pulled into the station, and I asked the attendant to replace the burned out signal bulbs.

Soon the station attendant was looking at me rather bemusedly, and he asked, "What did you want me to do?" I said, "Fix my turning lights, please." He said, "they are 100% all right! What do you mean, *fix* them?"

I got behind the wheel of the car, and I clicked the left turn (blink-blink-blink); I clicked the right turn (blink, blink, blink); they were in perfect working order.

My wife turned to Paul and said, "Hey, you really *do* heal automobiles!" Paul answered with a smile, and said, "Sure. I told you I would, didn't I?"

We got back in the car and had only driven a bit further when it began to rain. My wife had just had her hair done the day before, and, of course, she wanted to look glamorous for the weekend outing in Minneapolis, so she said, "Oh no, my hair! My hair is going to get ruined when we leave the car to go into the hotel."

Paul asked, "Oh, do you want it to stop raining?" Marilyn said, "Yes! Absolutely!" and so Paul said okay — *and it stopped raining.*

Marilyn said, "I don't believe that." Paul shrugged. "All right, you'd rather have rain." And it started raining again.

Marilyn said, "No, no, if you're going to make a thing out of it, I'd rather have sunshine." Paul said, okay, and the sun came out again.

Whether that was all a series of extraordinary coincidences, I'm not prepared to say, but let us say that if it was a matter of synchronicity, the coincidental timing was most impressive and made a most extraordinary kind of effect.

Paul turned to Marilyn after he had been turning the rain on and off and asked, "What would you like now?" We passed a furniture store just then, and Marilyn said, "How about a new dining room set?"

Paul laughed and said, "That will have to be up to Brad!" Well, okay, Brad takes a little longer to work his miracles, but Marilyn, you will be happy to hear, finally did get her new dining room table and chairs.

Oh, there are so many moments I could share! How do you sit down and sift out experiences with a man like Paul Twitchell? There was a time for a period of nearly a year when we talked on the telephone on an average of every other day. Many of these conversations were of a very deep, philosophical, metaphysical nature. Others were just because Paul wanted to talk to somebody or I wanted to talk to somebody or we wanted to commiserate with one another about the way that something might be going. Sometimes Paul had seen an article of mine or a book of mine, and he would just call and say, Hey, good job on that or hey, I like that. He was an enormously thoughtful man.

Paul Twitchell was also an enormously well-read man. I found it impossible to bring up a subject about which Paul did not know something and could not express an intelligent opinion. Now, you will often run into the parlor bluffers, as I call them — the person who tries to fake it whether you bring up topics esoteric or mundane. Paul was not bluffing. I know that he read at least ten to twelve different newspapers every day. I know that he read 50, 60, to 100 magazines every month, from all over the world.

We had a number of running jokes going between us. One was due to my liking an after-dinner cigar or pipe. I only smoke once or twice a day, but I like that after-dinner cigar. Because of the time differential, Paul would very often call after dinner, which would be like 7 o'clock our time and 5 o'clock Paul's time in California; and he would often catch me with my after-dinner cigar. Paul as you know, was not keen on smoking. He knew that I was an extremely moderate smoker, so he never chided me about it, but he always had this thing about not smoking when he was around. I found it impossible to keep my cigar lit when I was talking to Paul. I would take a big puff, and it was almost as if Paul could smell it and reach his finger out to twik off the ash — because when I would take the next puff, it would be out! I would light my cigar and start in again, and it would go out. Well, after a few times of this, of course, I made a joke out of it and Paul made a joke out of it, but I've always wondered if that old soul traveler was not zipping out and snuffing the fire in my cigar!

Another running joke was, again, due to the time differential. Paul's telephone calls would very often catch me in the shower. He was always apologetic, but this happened so often that my youngest, Julie, one time remarked when I stepped out of the shower all dripping wet to hang up the receiver, "Daddy, how is it that Paul Twitchell always knows when you are taking a bath?"

On one occasion I took a friend who was interested

14

in metaphysical subjects along with me to an ECK seminar in Chicago. He made an observation that I have since noticed for myself at the World Wide Seminars which I have attended. We sat through a number of lectures that evening and when the presentations had been completed, my friend turned to me and said, "You know the one thing I notice more than anything else at this seminar? Every one looks so happy. Everyone looks so blissfully happy, as if he has found something to give him joy. I've never quite seen that in any other group of this sort that I have attended."

And he was right, because the presentations had ended for the evening, and people were walking about with very expansive smiles. I've noticed that "phenomenon" at the World Wide conferences that I have attended, and I think it is a marvelous testimonial to Paul and to you people involved in ECKANKAR and whatever it is that you have going for you. I hope that you, in tribute to Paul, will always retain that happiness and always keep those smiles on your faces.

I was never a chela. I was never an ECK initiate. I was never a student of Paul's in the formal sense of the word. But I was a friend, and I valued Paul Twitchell's friendship, and it is as a friend that I shall miss him. I wish Darwin Gross, the new ECK master, the best of good accomplishments, good direction, good teaching, good enlightenment. I surely wish the best to all of those of you who have embraced the philosophy of ECKANKAR.

I said at the very beginning of my book, IN MY SOUL I AM FREE, that Paul Twitchell was an enigma to me. On the one level he remained an enigma and maybe that is the way it is to be between a man such as Paul Twitchell and a reporter, an observer, a historian, such as myself.

But on another level, he was not an enigma — he was a friend.

Brad Steiger
Decorah, Iowa

PART I

1. The Enigma
of Paul Twitchell

Paul Twitchell is an enigma.

Perhaps I must qualify that statement by saying that Paul Twitchell is an enigma to *me*. To hundreds of thousands of people in nearly every country in the world, Paul Twitchell is guru, teacher, master, soul traveler, and spiritual adept. Yet, in spite of the fact that I have included chapters on Twitchell in three of my books, written magazine articles about his work, and have now completed his biography, I must confess that the central core, the basic essence, of the man escapes me.

Maybe that is as it must be with such charismatic figures as Paul Twitchell. Perhaps those who work on the spiritual planes transcend the efforts of those journalists who attempt detailed chronicles of their lives. Now this is not to say that I fully believe all that I have been told about Twitchell by those who fervently feel that he has dramatically interacted with their lives. And this is certainly not to say that I comprehend the full range of the mysticism involved in the guru's philosophy of Eckankar.

Let me tell you something about my approach to the whole field of the paranormal. Book publishers often blurb me on the back covers as being an "internationally recognized authority on the occult and the paranormal." Such a statement, besides being ego-gratifying, is true to the extent that my books are published widely both here and abroad and that I have made a twenty-year study of psychic phenomena and the occult. But, you see, the key word here is "study": I am an outsider to the inner world of psychic and mystical machinery. To be certain, in the course of my studies I have seen things and heard things and experienced things which would seem to be beyond the ken of the average person; but I have not, with few notable exceptions, been in any way *personally* involved with or psychically responsible for any of the paranormal phenomena which I have reported. I do not, then, read the Tarot cards, or predict the future, or commune with the shades of those who have crossed over to the other side. I do accept the reality of non-physical man, and I do hold that man is more than chemical reactions, glandular responses, and conditioned reflexes, but you will have set yourself an exhaustive task if you should attempt to pin me down to any one approach, any single school of thought, or any specific dogma.

I must remain eclectic in my approach to the world of the paranormal if I am to be of any service to my readers. The moment that I believe too strongly in any one theory, then I shall attempt to force every encountered scrap of psychic experience into that pet hypothesis. If this should occur, my objectivity would be destroyed, and I should become worthless as an investigator. I should become the "true believer" and not the searcher, the explorer of the strange, the unusual, and the unknown, who sets forth on his voyage into the paranormal with an open and inquiring mind.

And this statement of personal credo has led us, by a briefly circuitous route, to Sri Paul Twitchell and Eckankar.

"ECK, which is the short label for Eckankar," Paul told me, "is not a yoga, religion, or philosophy, nor a metaphysical or occult system. It is merely a way to God-realization via soul travel."

Soul travel, according to Twitchell, is the natural means of going to God, and as such creates a joyous state in which one lives for all concerned — his family, mankind, and God.

The adept stands foursquare against the use of hallucinogenic drugs, hypnosis, yoga, or other "artificial" means of reaching "God-consciousness."

It is each man's responsibility to live in God-realization as much as possible without losing any of its effects in his daily personal life,"Sri Paulji said. "Because of this fact, it is only reasonable that we take the way that God has provided for us and not the way that man wants to take to get there faster by artificial agents. If man relies on such methods, all life becomes an illusion; he loses his responsibility to life, and he becomes a burden to society."

Although I realized that I was treading on rather dangerous ground, I suggested that the Maharishi Mahesh Yogi with his philosophy of "transcendental meditation" claimed also to offer a direct, simple, and natural route to enlarging the mind.

Twitchell replied calmly, in that gentle voice of his that seems to retain just enough of a southern accent to remind his listener that the adept does indeed inhabit a physical body, as well as travel about on the spiritual planes.

"Transcendental meditation is nothing but a mind exercise," Paulji said. "It is far too passive for the Western mind. Most of these Eastern teachings are very clearly designed for the Eastern manner of living, where a hot climate and widespread poverty is conducive to contemplation and inactivity.

"Transcendental meditation seems to offer some kind of spiritual welfare program. Most of these people who are putting their dollars into the Maharishi's bank account expect some kind of miracle to be done for them. Those who sincerely attempt this kind of meditation will soon find that this sort of thing is definitely not for everyone. It is not to be fooled with. So many of these people who are attracted to transcendental meditation are borderline neurotics to begin with, and a few sessions of this intense concentration will send them way out!

"The mind cannot really be expanded. Many of these people who practice transcendental meditation are only going to increase their own neuroses. Schizophrenia is a very great danger in this kind of Indian meditation."

I indicated that I could not agree with him more, and I asked Twitchell how Eckankar differed from transcendental meditation. Eckankar also draws upon certain Tibetan and Indian philosophies and reveres Himalayan holy men.

"For one thing," Paulji said, "we stay away from flabby-minded people. The *chela* [student] must apply himself to ECK for two years before he is initiated.

"For another thing, Eckankar is active, not passive. There is no sitting on a mountain top for twenty years contemplating navels. We do not make the error of confusing the microcosm with the macrocosm.

"And perhaps the most important difference is that in Eckankar we work toward the *chela's* developing complete spiritual freedom, total awareness, and total responsibility. The Indian meditation method currently garnering a great deal of publicity does not grant its *chelas* freedom. It retains its hold on the individual. When the student of Eckankar has completed his course of study, he is free to ask me to accept the role as his master or he is free to go his own way. The Indian masters demand a hold that lasts for the life of the student.

"It is the way of Eckankar that the individual must be free to accept his own responsibility and to stand on his own feet. There is no 'dropping out' of society in Eckankar. We seek to improve the social order, not to retreat from its responsibilities."

Although we will seek to define Eckankar at much greater length within the text of the book, we have, then, this capsule definition to work with for the present: "Eckankar is the key to freedom. Spiritual freedom is the key to heaven. Only when man loosens and lets go does he find himself guided to liberation of soul. Hence comes total freedom, total awareness, and total responsibility."

Now one of the basic premises in Eckankar is that one can more readily achieve this God-realization through travel in the soul body. What Sri Paul Twitchell is saying, in other words, is that he can be in more than one place at the same time. He says, and he has those who will testify to the validity of such statements, that he has been attending the theatre with his wife at the same time that he has been on the speaker's platform delivering a lecture in another part of the city. There are *chelas* in England, New Zealand, Nigeria, Sweden, and almost any other point on the globe, who claim that Sri Paulji ministers to them in the soul body while his physical body lies reclining at his San Diego home. By the same token, Paulji claims that the Tibetan masters of Eckankar visit him in their soul bodies from their *ashrams* and monasteries in the Himalayas.

During the course of researching this book on Sri Paul Twitchell and his Eckankar movement, I must have read at least two thousand letters from *chelas* and critics, searchers and skeptics from all over the world. Some letters testified to seemingly miraculous healings; some told of mysterious visitations from Paulji's soul body; and some relayed incidents that seem straight out of a bizarre "twilight zone" on the fringe of reality. Now, in all fairness, I must state herewith that in all cases I have read the *originals* of these letters, complete with original envelopes and postmarks. Twitchell has been unbelievably open in allowing me complete access to his files, and when I quote from a letter in this book, be assured that I am often squinting my eyes to decipher an off-beat handwriting style. In no case when I would ask, for example, for letters testifying to healing, would I receive a packet of retyped letters from anonymous requestees. In all cases, I have read the original of the letter from which I quote.

Here is a bit of correspondence that should make the most rigid of skeptics entertain at least a fleeting second thought about the true nature of the universe.

In late February of 1966, a Mr. W.R. of New York City wrote to Paulji to inquire about the adept's book *The Far Country.* Sri Twitchell wrote a polite note stating that the book was still in manuscript form.

On March 4th, Mr. W.R. wrote the adept a puzzled note. How could *The Far Country* still be in manuscript form, he wanted to know. ". . . It so happens that I have already seen this book in print at _____'s Occult Bookstore in this city. . . . There is a picture of Rebazar Tarzs [an ECK master] in the front of book." Mr. W.R. stated that surely Twitchell meant to say that the book was to be reissued, not published for the first time.

Twitchell again replied that *The Far Country* was still in the works and that Mr. W.R. could not possibly have seen the volume in a bookstore.

An incredulous Mr. W.R. gave additional details in his letter of March 11th:

"Your comments on my letter regarding *The Far Country* were just too fantastic for me to believe.

"You said I actually saw a manifestation of the book and Rebazar Tarzs' own picture . . . and that the books dissolved back into the ether again.

"Here is what actually happened: The owner walked right over to the section on Tibet and climbed up the ladder and handed me a copy. I then checked the price . . . then went up the ladder with the book and looked at the other two. . .

"I then opened the book and saw Rebazar Tarzs' picture on the frontispiece. He was shown from the chest up. He had quite a wide face and was pictured wearing some sort of headdress. The first page told how the book was dictated to Paul Twitchell of San Diego, California.

". . . I decided to pick up the book a few weeks later, as I didn't have enough money to pay for the book at the time. When I returned a few weeks later, all the copies were gone.

Now, do you mean to tell me that the book materialized to the store owner, who, in turn, handed it to me?

"Assuming this happened (and I don't believe it did), why should it happen to me, of all people? It hasn't done me any good, and it has put me to the bother of checking every occult bookstore in the city.

"At present I have four or five large book dealers all over the country making a search for me . . . Are you sure *you* are the one who doesn't remember that your book has already been published?"

Mr. W.R.'s book dealers drew blanks, of course, for *The Far Country* had not yet been printed. I shall publish excerpts from its text in a chapter of this book, which will truly mark the mysterious volume's first *physical* materialization.

Now, obviously, Mr. W.R. is reporting a valid experience of some kind. His tone becomes downright indignant toward the close of his letters, and who can blame him? He actually saw and held what he believed to be a copy of *The Far Country*. It becomes more than his mind can grasp when Sri Paul Twitchell tells him that the book is still in manuscript form and therefore he could not have browsed through a copy in a New York bookstore.

The 1966 postmarks are there for anyone to see. To say that Paulji and Mr. W.R. cooked up this little episode for my benefit is to say that over a year before I had even heard of Paul Twitchell, the adept envisioned my writing a book on him in 1968 and began to prefabricate some exciting little anecdotes for the text. In any event, I am left with two equally fantastic hypotheses: (1) In 1966 Mr. W.R. actually saw and held a copy of a book that had not yet, in 1968, been published; or (2) Paul Twitchell cannot only see the future but he can also manipulate it. If I have a choice, I will take the "accident" on the space-time continuum which apparently happened to Mr. W.R.

Here is another reported incident that will not set easy with those who like the security of a well-ordered physical universe.

A Mrs. A.F.S. of Pompano Beach, Florida, wrote a letter of inquiry to Sri Paul Twitchell. "Your book, *Introduction to Eckankar*, was suddenly handed to me one night by a man whom I did not know and who was silent. After handing me the book, he disappeared before my eyes! Have you written more on this subject? I find no price on the book, and would like more information."

Mrs. A.F.S. later saw Paulji's picture in the printed literature which was sent in response to her letter, and she wrote to Twitchell's secretary to express her astonishment that *Sri Paul Twitchell* had been the silent man who had handed her the book, then disappeared back into the etheric planes.

Admittedly such an experience is a bit difficult to accept if you tend to view the world through chemical test tubes and evaluate all your experiences on the bases of mathematical formulae. I found yet another such letter to be most fascinating and certainly indicative of something very alien co-existing with life as we ordinarily live it. Again, this letter came from an individual who had never before heard of Paul Twitchell until his name was given to her by her master while they were walking together on the inner planes. The name of the spiritual friend, she said, was Gopal Das [one of the holy men of Eckankar; I have his picture, which was sent to me by Paulji, before me now as I write this].

According to Miss R.F.C., Gopal Das suggested that she write to Twitchell. She replied that she would need Sri Twitchell's full name and address, and the holy man told her that it would be given to her. The next day, she picked up a copy of *Fate* magazine and opened it to the page containing Twitchell's ad.

Miss R.F.C. put off writing to Twitchell, however, because in the cold light of morning she could not help wondering whether her imagination had taken over her reason. Two days later, according to Miss R.F.C., Gopal Das and another master appeared to her and berated her for her failure to contact Paulji.

"True to my sex," Miss R.F.C. wrote, "I came up with several excuses (good ones, too, I thought). I was sure you would be convinced that I am a member of the 'lunatic fringe' but I was told to give you the name 'Rebazar.' I don't know if this is a person or place, or even if it is spelled properly, since I wrote it in the dark." ("Rebazar" would, of course, be the aforementioned Rebazar Tarzs, Paul Twitchell's personal spiritual adviser.)

Miss R.F.C. told Paulji that she had been practicing soul travel ever since she could remember, and that Gopal Das had always called her his little "sky-walker." Gopal Das had also told her to mention "Elenckar" when she wrote to Twitchell.

If this letter is spontaneous (and again, I cannot prove in any way that it is not, as it was written long before I had any interest in Twitchell or in Eckankar), it would seem to demonstrate the reality of such mysterious masters as Gopal Das and Rebazar Tarzs, who possess the talent of traveling great distances in their soul bodies. If it is a hoax, then it was, again, perpetrated with the precognitive knowledge that some day in the future Brad Steiger would describe the experience in a book. If Gopal Das and Rebazar Tarzs are creatures of illusion or hallucination, then it is indeed strange that a man on the West Coast and a woman on the East Coast should share the same hallucinatory figures, and that each should claim a long-standing intimacy with them, in the woman's case since childhood.

As Al Jolson used to say, "You ain't seen nuttin' yet!"

When I was asked to write this book, I really had no idea whether or not Paul would consent to such a project. I had featured him in a brief chapter in one of my anthologies and this very cursory examination of his work had brought a great deal of mail both to the publisher and to Twitchell's own office. I profiled his reading of the Akashic records of his clients' past lives in a book on reincarnation and reader response flooded both the publisher's office and my post office box, and brought Twitchell as many as 600 letters a week. It had become obvious that Paulji had a charismatic "something," but it still remained an open question whether or not Twitchell would permit a more extensive examination of his work.

"Do you think Twitchell will give his permission?" my agent asked when he called me that morning from New York. "I've done a fast job of selling on this book and I have to have a letter from Twitchell indicating his consent to show the editor, like yesterday!"

"Great," I groaned. "Paul has just left for a spiritual retreat in Mexico over the holidays."

"Try to reach him," he insisted. "We've got to have that letter from him."

"Look," I tried again. "Only Paul's private secretary and I have his unlisted number. He has to keep it that way or he would never get any rest. I don't think I will be able to reach him until he returns from Mexico in two weeks."

He mumbled something, and I had a mental image of my nervous agent lighting another cigarette and wishing that just this one time he had not been such a good salesman. "We've got to have that letter," he sighed. "Do your best."

I tried Paul's unlisted number on the off chance that he had not yet left for Mexico. No answer. I tried periodically during the day, then, toward evening, I got lucky. Gail, Paul's wife, was still in San Diego. The adept had decided to hold a seminar in Dallas before dropping on down to Mexico for the spiritual retreat. He would stay over in Dallas a few days, then return for Gail and head south for the *ashram*.

At 11:00 P.M. that night, Paul called me from Dallas and I outlined the project and told him what I would need from him. He readily agreed to the book and guaranteed his full cooperation.

The next morning when I called my agent the nervous edge was no longer in his voice. "It was the strangest thing," he said. "This morning as I lay in bed mentally debating the advantages and disadvantages of getting out of bed, I had the distinct impression that someone had entered my bedroom. When I looked up, I saw a rather fuzzy outline of a smiling man standing at the foot of my bed. 'Don't worry,' he said, 'I've given Brad permission to do the book.' Then he disappeared."

I was stunned by what I had just heard. This man is by no means insensitive, but let's face it, he is a literary agent, and to survive in the New York publishing world, he has to be a materialist, not a mystic.

"What did your visitor's voice sound like?" I asked.

"An unusual accent," he said. "Kind of like an Englishman talking with a Southern accent."

27

"That was Paul Twitchell," I had to say.

Paul Twitchell is an enigma.
In retrospect, perhaps the agent had only been dreaming. Perhaps I had allowed my excitement to momentarily shatter my shield of objectivity. Or had Paulji really appeared to my agent to assure him that all would be well?

Over the past few months I have read letters from Roman Catholic nuns seeking advice about matters in the convent, businessmen praising the adept for sound economic advice, the afflicted thanking Paulji for alleviating their suffering, accomplishing a healing, or implementing recovery from serious surgery.

A Mrs. K.B. in Michigan wrote to testify that, on several occasions, she had sat down to write to Paul about a matter that was troubling her only to find a reply in the mail before she had even had time to send her letter. She claimed also to have caught "glimpses" of the adept in his soul body.

Excerpts from other letters would include such statements as these:

"For the first time in years I have been able to sleep well. I thank you for your wonderful help." *London, England*

"After the first discourse I have been able to leave my body and visit many wonderful places in the spiritual worlds. God bless you for showing me the way through your wonderful course, the Illuminated Way." *Edinburgh, Scotland*

"I saw you and talked with you the other evening; you were concerned with my spiritual progress and I was talking with you about this. We were both outside the physical body. I was in my home, knowing that your physical body was on the Pacific Coast. What are these strange powers that you have?" *Denver, Colorado*

"I had this experience of standing outside my body

and looking down at it. You were with me saying that there was nothing to fear. Bless you, dear Master." *Devon, England*

"You visit me every afternoon in your spiritual body, between the hours of three and five, and discuss my spiritual progress." *Penang, Malaysia*

"When my daughter was injured, I found you beside me, saying to be calm. For the first time in my life there was no fear, instead love and the urge to get her help at once. It was so easy that I am amazed. She is improving, thanks to your help!" *Chicago, Illinois*

"It took me seven months to learn the key to soul travel under you, but now I can travel almost anywhere." *Brussels, Belgium*

Paul Twitchell is an enigma.

Has this man with his philosophy of Eckankar and his talk of inner planes, spiritual travelers, Akashic records, and soul bodies touched upon some ancient truths that really work for himself and for his initiates?

I asked Mrs. Doris Atkins of Burbank, California, why she believed in Eckankar and in the works of Paul Twitchell.

"ECK to me is a sacred assurance of inner knowing," Mrs. Atkins said. "It touches the depth of my heart and transcends me into a world not physical. My soul soars freely and rapturously into dimensions of like affinity. Part of ECK, to me, is my guru, Paul Twitchell. Such humility as he possesses can only be accepted, never rationalized. Sometimes when I am near him, I have a feeling of empathy. I actually don't think that a person could be near Mr. Twitchell without sensing that shining light."

Mrs. Alice Illouska of London, England, told me that she has felt happier and lighter and assured that she is now "on the right path to God" since she started her Eckankar lessons.

"I think Paul Twitchell is the main phenomenon in our age," Mrs. Illouska said. "I can't find words in English, nor in my native Greek, to describe the man. I have no doubt that he is gifted with special powers and exceptional qualities to help mankind. His brain is a limitless source of knowledge, as I have found there is no subject with which he is not acquainted.

"Just before Christmas a member of my family fell very seriously ill. We had four doctors to see the patient. This was the fourth attack of its kind in the last two years and the doctors were uncertain in their diagnoses. Nevertheless, the patient was crying and moaning, so I wrote at once to my good Mr. Twitchell.

"On New Year's Eve, while the patient was suffering and unable to sleep from pain, Mr. Twitchell was with us. I was in my bedroom all alone, resting on an armchair, when I heard a strange noise in the room . . . when I stood up, I felt someone touching my shoulder in a protective manner.

"I went to the patient's room soon after to find the patient smiling for the first time in nine days. The patient, too, had heard a strange noise in his room, as if someone had been walking near the bedside. Soon after the noise had ceased, the pain had started to go away, and to this day it has not returned.

"What I like about Mr. Twitchell is the quiet way he talks and the fact that he is not fanatic in his statements. Fanaticism breeds hatred. Mr. Twitchell makes no distinctions of religion and he told me that people of all nations and creeds can exercise Eckankar as a way to contact God.

"When Mr. Twitchell came to London, I went to see him for the first time at his Kensington Hotel. Before I had even talked to the receptionist, I heard a voice from behind me saying, "Hello, Alice!" and Paul Twitchell was coming straight toward me. The hotel was full of people coming and going. How did he know me? I do not know because we had never met previously. But he knew me all right!"

Mr. and Mrs. Klaus J. Ylinen of Stockholm, Sweden, testified that they had been spiritual seekers for many years.

"It has been a great relief to meet with the Eckankar movement and with Paul Twitchell himself," Klaus said. "Eckankar makes an enlargement of consciousness, refines the sensibilities, and teaches man how to live fully both in flesh and spirit.

"Paul Twitchell clears up the smoggy spiritual air and makes Eckankar—the old science of soul travel—seem very much like a modern, logical science, understandable for those of the Western world who have the capacity for it and who are able to absorb it. There is no need anymore for soul travel to be a mysterious and secret science."

Mrs. N.V. Muralt of Zurich, Switzerland, expressed her reluctance to give an opinion on a person who was spiritually superior. "One senses his strong personality and radiation, even though he is unobtrusive and rather reserved in his bearing," she said. "In private circles he does not mention his particular abilities, which appeals to me. I believe, and hope, that ECK will be one of the few possibilities to prove to our science and to our present world in quite a methodical and verifiable manner that the core of man is spiritual and indestructible, that there is a future life and a divine spiritual significance to all of life."

Eckankar is the path to God, the *Sugmad*, in the view of Miss Mary W. Hirdler of Santa Monica, California.

"How do I use Eckankar during a busy work schedule? Frankly, I could not get through the day without it," said Miss Hirdler. "ECK gives me inner peace, an attitude of thankfulness, and energy to get to the point of completion and feeling of accomplishment.

"There are times when Eckankar principles help me with the healing power for people, situations, and conditions. Paul Twitchell is with me. I do not need to call; I acknowledge his presence. By uniting spiritual power we are channels for healing. He directs it to me and I let it flow.

"Recently I went to the dentist for some minor work and used an Eckankar method for soul travel. By being out of the body I was not aware of pain and fear. My dentist thought I had had a nap, but I had projected my consciousness to Japan and had enjoyed the serenity, beauty, and fragrance of a garden.

"There is much publicity today about prayer and meditation. My comment is, don't tell God what to do! Listen! Obey! Act! I can listen while I do what is planned for the day, but it requires much discipline and practice. This is important for growth and development. It is important, also, to release the thoughts and tensions of each day. Techniques and methods are followed for inner peace, rest, and sleep as required.

"Eckankar is an ancient science. Paul Twitchell is not teaching something new. He is making us more *aware* of the Truth as we awaken, develop, and unfold. He answers the questions we need to know. He loves us with understanding and freedom. He is a teacher who does not possess his *chelas.* There is a bond without bondage. We are united in spirit and purpose. We serve God by letting Him express himself through us. Eckankar is the path to God, the *Sugmad*; a God I can trust and depend on. I accept God as my creator, my source of happiness and joy. This is shared with Paul and *all* who accept truth and responsibility."

2. A Stormy Petrel

Since that day when Paul Twitchell hammered the
pane glass out of the front door with tiny, bloody,
three-year-old fists in protest to his having been
locked in, he has always been an authentic,
nondescript individualist who loves his freedom and
independence.

It was Kay-Dee, Paul's sister, who bandaged his
wounds that day, and it would be she who would
prove to be his ally throughout his childhood. Time
and time again, it would be young Paul and teenaged
Kay-Dee who would square off against Mom and
Clyde in domestic quarrels that ranged in seriousness
from plucking the tail feathers of Pliny, Mom's
parrot, to practicing exercises in soul travel, a means
of transportation to which Mom was bitterly
opposed.

As a small child, Paul was told that Mom, a proud,
stern, half-Chickasaw Indian beauty, was his
stepmother and that Kay-Dee and Clyde were his
stepbrother and stepsister. A boy in a sleepy southern
town like China Point did not bother to figure out
that if Kay-Dee, who was ten years older, and Clyde,
who was four years older, were the products of his
father's former marriage, then Mom would have to be
his real mother, not his stepmother. Or if Kay-Dee
and Clyde were her children and Paul was the child of
a former marriage, he would have to be the oldest
child, not the youngest. It would not be until he was
a teenager that Grandmother Twitchell would set the
lad straight. A wealthy matriarch who ruled her
family and its pursestrings with an iron hand, Grands

believed that her high-stepping son had fathered the boy, who had been born out of wedlock on a Mississippi riverboat, and she forced the prodigal to take the infant into his family. Her son had to admit that it was entirely within the realm of possibility that he could, indeed, be the lad's father, so he acquiesced to the demands of his wealthy mother. After all, he had reasoned, what was another mouth to feed as long as Grands provided the wherewithal?

Effie, Paul's "mother," although as stoic as her Indian forebears in such matters as physical pain, was unable to accept the boy's presence with the same outward calm that she might have been able to maintain toward a broken leg. Paul, whether or not he was the seed of her husband's extra-marital union with another woman, served as an ever-present living, breathing reminder that her man was openly unfaithful to their marriage vows.

"My foster father loved his family dearly," Paul remembered, "but he was very much interested in stepping high. He traveled a lot—on riverboats, on trains, and, in his later years, on airplanes. He had a tremendous amount of energy and could do the work of five men at one time. He was always on the go representing his company, because he was known as a highly intelligent man who could drive a hard bargain in business. He was also considered an extremely honorable person. His integrity was beyond question.

"While my father was always enthusiastically involved in living, my mother seemed indifferent to life," Twitchell reflected. "Why these two people stayed together is beyond me."

Paul remembers his mother as being cruel in her punishment of the children, especially him, whom she had as little to do with as possible. "The very fact that she had to raise me was a hard pill for her to swallow," Paul said, "and it affected her attitude toward life. She believed that she had been trapped,

34

and she bitterly fought the way that my father, Kay-Dee, and I believed."

Clyde, Paul's brother, the middle child of the Twitchell family—the second child and the youngest of the union between them—was the mother's favorite. She carefully nursed him to cherish her beliefs and to side with her on every domestic issue that came up. Clyde was tall, dark-eyed and swarthy of complexion. He cared for little other than athletics, hunting, and fishing. He was extremely quiet, seldom spoke to anyone, and would eventually fight his way up through company politics to take over the senior Twitchell's position upon his retirement.

"My father had learned something about soul travel when he was in Europe at one time," Paul said. "He made the acquaintance of Sudar Singh and the two of them hit it right off. The Indian holy man taught him some of the elementals of soul travel and the two of them corresponded frequently. I know now for a fact that Sudar Singh visited him regularly in the *Nuri Sarup* [the light body]. Father taught Kay-Dee some of the basic steps in soul travel, and it was these elementary lessons that saved my life when I was five years old."

What had begun as a simple chest cold had developed into an acute case of pleurisy, and young Paul's lungs were rapidly filling with fluid. The boy moaned for release from the fiery torment of his fever. He called for his father to bring him a glass of cool water.

"Your father is across the ocean," his mother told him. "Right about now he's probably in some fancy restaurant sipping some chilled champagne. I'll just bet he's not alone, either!"

The woman's face, darkly beautiful, remained impassive to the suffering of the boy lying in his pain on the bed before her. "I'll bring you a drink," she said at last.

35

"How's the kid?" Kay-Dee asked, returning from school with an armload of books. She was fifteen, slender, budding into lovely young womanhood.

Mrs. Twitchell turned from the faucet where she was filling a glass of water, shrugged. "He's no better, probably worse."

"What did the doctor say?" Kay-Dee demanded. "He must have been more specific than that!"

"The doctor says Paul is very sick. If he does not pass the crisis tonight, he will die."

Kay-Dee caught at her lower lip, blinking back the tears that stung her eyes. "You don't seem terribly concerned," she accused her mother.

"Of course I am concerned," the woman snapped. "After all, he's your father's son, or so Grands would have us believe! But I'm no healer. I can't cure the boy by waving my hands over him. Perhaps if he were stronger, like Clyde, he wouldn't have got sick in the first place."

Kay-Dee took the glass from her mother's hand. "I'll take Paul his water," she said.

As soon as the teenaged girl stepped into her younger brother's room, she could see that he hovered on the very edge of death and that this night might be his last. She put her hand on the boy's forehead and felt the terrible fever. An audible gurgle came from within his chest.

"Hey, kid," she whispered, trying to make her voice as cheery as possible. "Here's your water."

But little Paul had lapsed into a fitful sleep. Kay-Dee recoiled when it occurred to her that Paul might never again open his eyes.

"The doctor says he can't help you, and Mom says she can't help you," Kay-Dee said resolutely, "but maybe *I* can help you, kid!"

Desperately she performed a mental review of the exercises which her father had given her in how to get out of the body and how to heal via soul projection.

"If only I can do it when Dad isn't here to help me," Kay-Dee said, closing her eyes in silent prayer. "But I must try. I know it is what Dad would want me to do!"

Late that night, Kay-Dee slipped into Paul's room. She knew that if her mother knew that she was going to try to heal by soul travel, she would take the switch to her.

She sat down beside her younger brother's bed and assumed the lotus posture. She took a couple of deep breaths and slipped out of her physical body into the *Atma Sarup*, the soul body.

In her non-physical self, Kay-Dee was freed from the normal boundaries of time and space. She hovered briefly above the form of the suffering Paul, and then glided down to ease the boy out of his physical body. In an instant, the two soul bodies were hanging off the bedroom ceiling like a pair of ethereal eyes viewing the body on the bed below them.

"Where are we, Kay-Dee?" Paul asked, wondering. It was the first he had known of the amazing talent his sister possessed.

"We are in our soul bodies, Paul," Kay-Dee told him. "See there, below us, that is your physical body."

"Am I dead?" Paul asked.

"No," Kay-Dee said soothingly. "You are not dead. Do not be alarmed and do not be frightened. Do you feel the pain in your chest?"

"I—I feel fine," Paul answered. "But somehow I know that he—I mean, myself—down there on the bed *is* dying."

"Yes," Kay-Dee admitted. "But we are not going to allow that to happen. With all the might of my soul body, I am going to concentrate on your getting well. Help me. Think of good health . . . of recovery . . . of goodness and strength."

Within moments, Paul knew that all was well and

that the living clay lying on the bed below them would be his temple again. But then a strange reluctance seemed to possess him. He no longer wanted to return to his physical body with all its aches, pains, and minor miseries. How wonderful it would be to soar free of the flesh!

"You must return!" Kay-Dee scolded. "This is a temptation that you must fight."

"But I know now that I can travel anywhere that I want to," Paul said with a childish enthusiasm which betrayed his lack of wisdom. "And I can do anything I want to do. Nothing can stop me!"

But Kay-Dee had progressed enough in her spiritual studies to be able to handle the situation of a soul reluctant to return to its body. A powerful charge of concentration from her *Atma Sarup* sent the soul body of the exuberant Paul back to his physical form.

"The next thing I remember," Paul said, "is that I was awakening to find the family and our doctor standing by my bedside. The doc was saying something about a miraculous recovery, and Mother seemed surprised, impressed, and pleased. Even Clyde was grinning broadly. Kay-Dee only gave me a sly wink.

"Two weeks later, when Pop returned home, I heard him thank Kay-Dee for saving my life. It seemed that he had projected himself to the house from overseas for the same reason, only to find that Kay-Dee was taking care of things very nicely. From that time on, Kay-Dee began to instruct me in the basic exercises of soul travel."

Mom was bitterly opposed to these experiments in bilocation. She believed, purely and simply, that such works belonged in a category of experiences which were Satan's very own. Whenever she caught either Kay-Dee or Paul practicing bilocation, she went on the warpath and there would be a severe whipping in store.

"As might be expected," Paul recalled, "I got more than my share of sessions with her whip. She never spared that rod whatsoever. She and Kay-Dee used to have some bitter fights over me. If it hadn't been for Kay-Dee, I'm certain that I would have been cast out during one of the periods when my foster father was away.

"Of course, Grands Twitchell would not allow anyone to pick on me too much, either. And she kept a tight hold on the pursestrings to see that her word was abided by. She was a hard-boiled businesswoman who ran some fluorspar mines, mostly with a rifle; but nevertheless she made money out of them. The mines had been in the family for generations, and Grands took care of her end of the mining tradition. She had been widowed at an early age and had been left with five children to rear, but Grands brought them up and took care of them all."

It was during one of his summer visits to Grands' estate that young Paul had an unforgettable confrontation with the "thing" on Melpar Hill.

Everyone in the area knew that something haunted Melpar Hill, but just what it was nobody could describe. How it harmed those unfortunate enough to have been faced by it was more than the natives of the rural area wanted to talk about.

The folktales of the countryside in which Paul Twitchell grew up were rich in stories of ghosts, ha'nts, and things that walked by night. His teeth were sharpened on yarns about supernatural beings that stalked the hours of darkness. When nighttime came, he would hardly venture beyond the limits of the yard gate.

Grands had told him many times about the time when Grandpa had come home from the Civil War and had crossed the hill late at night. When Grandpa reached the edge of the rough road which led into the dark wilderness of trees on the hill, something had come out of the woods—a tiny thing, like a white lamb. It had fallen in behind Grandpa's horse and had trotted along quietly. Grandfather had pulled his revolver and waited for its attack.

It had blazing red eyes, and a strange, snarling sound occasionally broke from its throat. When the horse reached the center of the hill, it let out a weird cry of fright, for suddenly they were surrounded by what seemed to be a hundred shadowy little figures.

Grandpa had dug his spurs into the horse's flanks and began to race for the bottom of the hill with the shadowy entities snapping at his animal's heels. Whatever strange creatures from the haunted hill were pursuing them, they gave up the chase at the edge of the hill.

One summer day, young Paul decided that he would hike over to Melpar Hill to inspect those mysterious grounds of which he had so often heard. He made certain first that the sun was shining brightly, as even an overcast sky might tempt the ha'nts that dwelled on the hill.

Paul found only a few rattlesnake skins lying over arid earth and rocks to hold his interest until he discovered a cave with a few bones scattered on the floor. To his childish appraisal, the bones simply had to be human. When Paul emerged from the cave, he found to his dismay that he had underestimated two very important factors: the length of time it had taken him to walk the five miles to Melpar Hill, and the length of time he had spent exploring the eerie cave. It was now twilight.

The boy was frightened. He rushed out to the road and began trotting to gain time.

Then something came out of the woods. Its shape was unassuming enough; it appeared to be a small white lamb. It began to trot behind Paul, and that was when he noticed its wild, reddish eyes and heard the vicious snarl that it was making deep within its throat. The boy sped in terror through the lengthening shadows of twilight.

When the two reached the summit of the hill, the creature let out a strange call. Instantly there seemed to be hundreds of the small, white entities snarling and snapping at Paul. His feet picked up speed. He was over the hill and upon safe ground within seconds. Whatever had been following him stopped at the edge of Melpar Hill.

"The shape which these entities assumed is certainly unique in the annals of haunting," Twitchell said recently. "I don't think I have ever heard of any other case wherein ghostly, snarling lambs haunted an area. Even today, though, I am told, people who travel over the hill in automobiles will every now and then come up with a queer story about seeing white lambs on Melpar Hill at night."

Meeting the "thing" on Melpar Hill was a nightmarish experience, but it did not compare in shock effect to the knowledge which Paul gained in Grands' antebellum mansion in his fifteenth summer.

Grands had given Kay-Dee a choice of either two years in Paris or four years at the state university to decide whether or not she really did have any artistic talent. Kay-Dee had taken the long shot on Paris. Reading between the lines of her letters, Paul doubted very much if his sister was learning very much about art, but it was obvious that she was learning a great deal about life. Grands had also promised Paul a trip to Paris if he would maintain better than average marks during his four years of high school. With such a promise as incentive, Paul had polished off high school at the age of fifteen with top marks.

A week after graduation exercises, Grands telephoned Paul and summoned him to the big house in the country. It was a fine June morning when he went to see her. Jamie, the wrinkled old handyman, butler, and chauffeur, was mowing the lawn.

"Fine day, isn't it?" Jamie greeted him in his old-fashioned, grand manner. "Old Missus is waiting for you in the parlor."

Stepping into Grands' old mansion was like moving backward into an antebellum, *Gone-with-the-Wind* world. In the parlor, there were a couple of faded easy chairs that looked as if they might easily break apart if one sat in them. A yellowed leather settee was pushed into one corner, and some kind of drooping plant languished beside it. The north wall had a fireplace with a wide mantel, and on each side were bookshelves that reached upward to the ceiling.

It was in this room that Paul's voracious reading habits were born with the help of practically every member of the family. At the age of three, Paul's father had substituted the Zane Grey stories for Mother Goose tales as bedtime reading fare. The boy's imagination had been fired on gunfighters and spirited horses until Kay-Dee took umbrage at blood-and-thunder tales for such a young boy. Kay-Dee was at the age when she was promoting sophistication, and she had begun reading Shakespeare, Dickens, and the classics to the lad. It was a reproachful mother who had challenged this diet of reading and decided that the youngster needed Biblical readings. In rare moments of attention toward her foster son, she had taken time from her domestic duties to perform this task. Everybody had got into the act of shaping Paul's reading habits, except, of course, Clyde, who had not really cared whether Paul learned to read or fell in the Mississippi.

Grands was sitting in her usual position with the usual shot of whiskey in her hand when Paul entered the parlor. Grands' nose was a bit too large—she had always referred to it slyly as a Roman proboscis. Paul could not resist entertaining the slightly disrespectful notion that Grands looked very much like the eccentric W.C. Fields dressed in female attire.

"Come on in, boy," Grands bade him with a wave of the shot glass. She wore an old bathrobe and she had one hand thrust into a side pocket. Paul knew that that hand clutched a large roll of bills, which Grands always carried on her person as a reminder that she was secure in a merciless world. Grands had never trusted banks or bankers, although she had been forced to do business with them in her later years.

Her feet were covered by a pair of brown gaiters. Beside Grands' chair was a gold spittoon which was half-filled with tobacco juice. She had often told the story of how, when a young girl, her father had given her a choice of smoking a pipe or chewing, either of which was the fashion of the day for women. Grands had decided to chew, because she had deemed it to be a cleaner habit.

"You will recall, I am certain, that I made you a promise," Grands began in a strong, raucous voice. Her weight had easily shot up to one hundred and sixty pounds since she had got off her horse and into her Cadillac. "I promised you that if you kept your grades up you could go to Paris for a few weeks and visit your sister. You do recall that promise?"

Paul grinned, not minding the way Grands was teasing him. "Yes, Grands," he said. "I surely do recall your promise."

"Well," Grands said, slowly working at the wad of tobacco in her mouth, "it 'pears that you have kept your part of the bargain and now I'm a gonna have to keep mine."

Paul began to blurt his thanks, but Grands waved him silent. "Now you're going to have to do some spying for me while you're over there," Grands said. "More'n likely Kay-Dee is going to be too busy with them Frenchies to pay much attention to you, anyway. I figure my granddaughter has inherited some of my wild blood, so I pay no mind to that, but I do want you to see if she really has any kind of talent as an artist, 'cause I surely do not want to be wasting my money on her if she hasn't."

"Kay-Dee is a very good artist," Paul said in defense of his sister.

"Now don't you go siding with her until you've seen her paintings," Grands scolded. "You two are always siding with each other. You give them paintings a good inspection, and by the time you get back in late August, it'll be time you register for your freshman year at the state university."

Paul received the news that he would be attending college with a whoop of uncontrolled excitement. Paris and college! It was almost more than he could bear. He began to pour out his thanks to the stern old matriarch.

"Oh," she put him off, "I figure every young buck should see those foreign countries. I did myself once, a long time ago. But so many of them foreigners tried proposin' marriage to get my money, that I swore that if I made it back to China Point unhitched I would never leave the country again. Never have neither, 'cept a couple times for business reasons after I was married."

Grands got up stiffly, hobbled to the windows, and fiddled with the shutter cords. "Paul," she said softly, "there's something else that has to be said, and this seems like as good a time as any. Paul, you were born out of wedlock to a woman on a riverboat. I put the blame on your pop, and I've made him bring you up just like you was his own. He's never said one way or the other whether he is or he isn't, but I think he's been a pretty good father to you."

Paul stood a long time in silence. The news had dealt his youthful ego a severe blow, and his brain was having a difficult time making sense out of all the jumbled images that were crowding his consciousness, each one clamoring for attention.

"Then Pa never was married to my mother?"

"No. You're old enough to know how he is with women."

"Then that's why M—M . . . Effie hates me so."

"Effie doesn't hate you, boy, but maybe she's taken a lot of things out on you that she wishes she had been able to take out on your old man."

"And why Clyde has always been pounding on me ever since we were kids."

"There have been good times and bad. Same as any family," Grands pointed out. "Kay-Dee has always loved you and looked out for you, and so have I."

Grands held him in her arms. "You've been a real man to take all this without a whimper, Paul."

But Paul was not a man. He was fifteen, a boy who suddenly felt himself in a world of strangers.

"Who was my real mother?"

"Guess there's no harm in your knowing," Grands said. "Mrs. Folger is your mother, and she's got a family of her own now."

Paul jerked back at the name. Pretty Mrs. Folger, the social leader of China Point. He had often wondered why she had always been so friendly to him, and why his feelings toward her had been so unusually warm. His head was reeling. He thought he might become ill all over Grands' cherished antique furniture. He bade her good-bye and ran from the house.

That night he peeped through the windows at the Folger house and watched the woman who was said to be his real mother moving about her kitchen.

He went down to the roadside cafe where the Memphis-New Orleans truckers stopped over for meals. While a trucker was munching a hamburger, Paul crawled into the rear of his truck and hid himself. He slept most of the way to New Orleans.

A freighter was loading at one of the docks that next morning when he went down to the piers. Paul learned that the ship was bound for Haiti, and he was elated. He had a former classmate living there with his parents. They would be glad to see him.

The ship was three days out before the captain discovered his stowaway. He could do nothing but carry Paul to Port-au-Prince, his first port of call. Paul's friends sent him back to China Point by air.

When he walked into the old parlor again, Grands was sitting in the same old rocker, as if she had not moved. The usual slug of whiskey was in her gnarled hand, and the plugs of tobacco were at her elbow.

She stared at Paul solemnly with her icy gray eyes, and finally grunted: "How was the trip?"

"Kind of quick," Paul managed.

"Did you get some of the pain out?"

"Some."

Grands gnawed herself a chew of tobacco, let the cud roll around in her mouth, then spat a stream of amber juice at the spittoon. "It don't matter much about a kid's birth," she said, dabbing at her moist chin with a soiled lace handkerchief. "Maybe a small town like China Point has many faces, but the world don't really care much about any one person and all the injustices that he might think he has. You go off to Paris now and finish the job of forgetting.

"And just you remember this one thing. You try to make as much happiness out of this life as you can before you leave for the next world!"

3.   *On Gaining Spiritual Experience*

Paul had little time to get adjusted to Paris, to his sister's left-bank friends, or to Kay-Dee's brand of artistic expression before Pop cabled them from China Point that Mom was dying.

"I hate dying!" Paul complained loudly on that last morning when they went to the hospital. "I hate it! Why does it have to be her?"

Paul and his foster mother had had little use for one another, but the fact that death was cutting down this proud woman had upset him terribly.

"Take it easy, Paul," Kay-Dee whispered. "It's not easy for any of us."

"Paul!" his father called sharply. "Come on, we're ready to leave for the hospital!"

"Don't be too hard on him, Pop," Kay-Dee said. "He's hurting as much as the rest of us. It's that he's too sensitive to watch her die!"

Pop drove over to Broadway where he pulled into the parking lot behind the hospital. He got out and stood by the car in the bright summer sunlight. His Panama hat was pulled low over his forehead, and Paul could see that his eyes were glinted with grief. Clyde stood beside Pop, tall, dark, dressed in the black clothes he had learned to wear at the seminary where he was studying.

"Don't make a scene, Paul," his father said in a low voice. "I know you don't like it, but we've got to go through with it. Besides, she was a mother to you."

"Oh, cut it out!" Paul blurted. "She wasn't my mother, and you never acted like you loved her either!"

Clyde stepped between them. "I'm going to get you for this, Paul. Excuse me, Pop, but this little monkey needs some sense pounded into him. I hope that God will forgive him!"

"I don't need His forgiveness nor your prayers!" Paul snapped bitterly.

"Stop it, all of you," Kay-Dee said, putting her arm around Paul, standing slender and defiant against the men of the family. She was a handsome girl with a classic face. "Everybody's upset. Don't make it any worse. Mom's dying! Remember?"

Silently their father led the way into the hospital. They were ushered upstairs to the second floor along a corridor that smelled sharply of disease and cleaning fluid. Paul felt faint and he leaned against Kay-Dee, who took his hand and led him into an arid, narrow room where an awful stench of death hung.

The long cot showed only the pale shell of a woman with wide, black, staring eyes and sticks of arms hanging over the sheets. Recognition shone in her eyes as they gathered around the bed like a quartet of grim crows that had come to watch her die.

"Effie," Pop said in a sad whisper. "We're all here."

Her dark Indian eyes swept them in a chilling glance. Paul saw nothing but disdain in them for him. The woman had never had any use for her foster child.

"Well, so you are," she said in a whisper that sounded as if it had come from beyond the grave. "You've come to launch me from this place, eh?"

The rustle of a nurse's starched skirt diverted their attention from the near-corpse on the bed. The nurse picked up Mom's left hand and studied it. The hand

48

was badly swollen and her wedding band was embedded in the flesh.

"This ring is cutting off the circulation in your hand," the nurse spoke emphatically. "It must come off."

Mom blazed up against the act of taking from her the symbol that proved her fidelity to one man. It was a plain, broad, gold wedding band, but it signified that she was a married woman, even though her conjugal life had not been one of the kind of bliss reported by the women's magazines.

"I don't give a whoop for all your reasons for wanting it off," Mom snapped at the doctor who had come into the room to bolster the nurse's argument. "I want to keep my ring. I want to die with it on my hand!"

Her voice became a hoarse whisper. "I've stayed with a man for thirty years and fought out the battles of marriage, even though, sometimes, it wasn't worth the trouble. But this ring . . . is my link to this life . . . to this earthly world . . . and I'm not going to give it up so easily."

They all knew that she meant that the ring linked her with Clyde, her son, her favorite. She had molded him, guided him into the pattern of the man she had wanted in her life. She had taught him to shoot ducks and repair boats, and she had waded with him in the river bottoms in high boots and overalls while trapping or shooting game.

It had been Kay-Dee, backed by Pop's argument, who had finally got Clyde into a seminary to study preaching. Pop had just not been able to see any future for Clyde, outside of running around in the swamps killing game.

"This isn't going to hurt, ma'am," the nurse said indifferently as she picked up Mom's hand.

"It won't make much difference to a dying woman," Mom whispered. She was too weak to struggle any longer against the authority which had caught her in the last few hours of her life. And her proud Indian blood forbade her from asking any of her family to stop it.

"Can't you let it stay on?" Pop finally asked hoarsely.

"You heard what the doctor said," the nurse said without looking up. "It might help to keep the blood flowing freely."

When, after some struggle, the ring came off, the nurse set it on the bedside table with artificial cheerfulness and silently left the room.

All the while the nurse had been working on her ring, Mom had kept her unblinking gaze fastened on Paul. Now that the nurse had left, Mom gasped two words loud enough for all to hear: "You bastard!"

The words tore into Paul's guts. The guilt of his birth swept through him in a sickening wave of pain. He dropped his eyes to avoid her hot, hateful eyes.

At last Mom turned to Clyde, and her expression softened. She held love only for him.

Her face became a pale mask of lifeless flesh. She closed her eyes and appeared to be a manikin of clay, except for her rasping breath. She was preparing to make that crossing from which no traveler returned.

Paul could stand it no longer. Death was his foe. He hated death so much that it was no longer possible for him to stand there watching her die.

He crept backwards to the door. As he opened it, Mom's eyelids snapped wide and she gave him one last, stabbing glare. It stampeded him. He made it to the wicker chair in the vestibule and sat down, trembling. He tried to remember everything mean about her—the awful lashings that she had given him; the flat, mean voice which she had used to scold him; the terrible inner hurts which she had inflicted upon him. But nothing came from his memory. He was as blank as the flat, barren walls which surrounded him.

50

It was in this moment he realized that hatred was too great a burden to carry. He would try to remember only the love for Mom which he had stored up inside.

It was upon their return to Paris that Paul met Sudar Singh for the first time. The Indian holy man was lecturing in France in an effort to gain sincere disciples. When Kay-Dee introduced her brother to the bearded adept, Sudar Singh took Paul's hand in his own and looked warmly into his eyes.

"Your father told me to expect you," he said. "We had a rather long chat last night."

Paul knew that Sudar Singh was not referring to long-distance cable. Kay-Dee had told him that it had been Sudar Singh who had taught Pop the ancient art of soul travel that Pop had in turn relayed to her. Paul had been given the most convincing of demonstrations of bilocation when Kay-Dee had healed him of the near-fatal pleurisy, and he had himself practiced slipping out of the body since that time; but he remained a bit skeptical about the possibility of bilocation at such great distances.

"You mean Pop appeared to you in Paris last night?" Paul asked.

"On the contrary," Sudar Singh said, "I journeyed to China Point. It is so restful there and I needed to get away if only for a brief time, from the hubbub of Paris."

Paul decided to test the holy man. "Is that big grandfather clock in Pop's office still running five minutes behind time?"

Sudar Singh smiled. "The grandfather clock stands just off the vestibule in your home. There is no such clock in your father's office."

Paul was not yet satisfied. "That's the big one. I mean the smaller one in Pop's office."

Sudar Singh frowned, but then he laughed in a good-natured manner. "Why do you seek to test me, Paul? Why are we playing this game? I have been in your home many, many times. I can describe it as well as you. Both your father and I stood off and watched Kay-Dee heal you when you were five years old." Then, turning to Kay-Dee, Sudar Singh asked: "Is it possible that he does not know about these things? Has he seen, and not yet believed?"

"Paul is still a searcher," Kay-Dee said. "He knows of soul travel, but he, well, both of us, would like to learn more of the ancient science of soul travel. I have grown weary of trying to arrange my paints on canvas in a manner that attracts the eye of a critic or a buyer. I would rather spend the time trying to better arrange my life."

Sudar Singh was silent for several moments before he spoke. "Am I to understand that you would like to return with me to my spiritual retreat in Allahabad?"

"That is my wish," Kay-Dee said emphatically. "Paul?"

"Well," Paul shrugged, "it sure has been fun here in Paris. Grands told me to learn how to get some fun out of life. But maybe it's more important to find out what life is all about. I'll go where Kay-Dee goes."

Kay-Dee and Paul lived in Sudar Singh's *ashram* for nearly a year before the irate Grands managed to haul them home.

The wisdom which Paul acquired in this *ashram*, or spiritual retreat, has been carefully postulated in the discourses and exercises of Eckankar—some of which this author has received permission to present in subsequent chapters of this book. This was a time of study and meditation for Kay-Dee and Paul. It was also a time of great spiritual growth. To attempt a complete account of the day-by-day rituals of the *ashram* would prove much too esoteric for the general reader, so we shall, at this point in our narrative, pass over the months spent at the spiritual retreat and deal with the lessons learned throughout the course of this text.

This year in India was not spent totally in an attitude of holy learning. Paul had reached his sixteenth birthday, and he decided that he needed a furlough from the *ashram*. He traveled to Bombay, put up in a hotel, and then set out in search of a holy man who Sudar Singh had said was extremely wise in the ways of God.

"I headed for the rough, slum area of the city," Paul recalled, "for the old Hindu was said to live among the poor so that he might better give to people who truly needed his wisdom and advice. When he would venture out to minister to the wealthy, he would collect their old clothes so that he might distribute them to the poor upon his re-entry into the slums."

At last one scrawny, rough-looking fellow responded to Paul's inquiries and offered to take the young American to the holy man.

"Instead," Paul chuckled now in his recollection, "he took me to the house of a pseudo-swami who started in berating me for being a rich American."

While the teenaged Paul Twitchell sat there listening to the fanatical swami, he slipped out of his physical body to explore the other rooms in the ramshackle old house. In a room which appeared to be the kitchen, his soul body saw two evil-looking men with knives and a throttle rope. They were discussing in very explicit terms just exactly what they were going to do to the young American when he came through the hall to the door. Paul knew then that he had been set up by the rough-looking little man who had guided him to the phoney swami, and his soul body began to search for another exit by which his physical body might make its escape.

"It was a dark, evil old house with broken windows, and sections of its rooms were half in ruins," Paul said. "I found that there were two doors beside the front one—a side door and a back one, both apparently hanging off their hinges. The old swami must have been taking drugs, for he raved on for at least an hour before he dropped off into a doze. Every time I would try to get up, he would rouse himself and start ranting again.

"Finally he fell into a sound enough sleep so that I was able to get up, take off my shoes, and, keeping one eye on the thugs in the kitchen, tip-toe to the side door and run like crazy until I reached a decent-looking cafe. Two policemen were there, and I got the message across that some thugs were following me. They got a taxi for me and sent me to the hotel where I was staying."

Kay-Dee and Paul arrived home in China Point shortly before the outbreak of World War II. The United States still had not become involved in the shooting aspects of the conflict, so young Paul went to Canada and tried to enlist in the Canadian Air Force. He was rejected, but shortly after the sneak attack at Pearl Harbor brought America into the terrible conflagration that was consuming Europe and the Pacific, Paul enlisted in the U.S. Navy.

Twitchell followed the campaigns across Guam, the Philippines, Okinawa, and Japan. Paul had attained his full height of five feet, six inches, and had acquired the nickname of "Little Toughie."

On October 13, 1942, John Hix ran an item about Twitchell in his "Strange As It Seems" column for United Features Syndicate, Inc.: "The family of Paul Twitchell, U.S.N.R., has its name on the war record of every American war! He is the cousin of Robert Barret Winch, the first American killed overseas in World War I!"

Paul had many unique experiences during the war which enabled him to make full use of the spiritual science which he had acquired from Sudar Singh.

Once in the Pacific when the fleet was under attack by Japanese fighter planes, Paul was serving as gunnery officer with a small crew of men on a twenty-millimeter gun in one of the forward tubs aboard ship. A shell had jammed in the loading and the crew was trying to unlock the gun in order to extract the shell.

Suddenly Paul's father appeared at his side. "Get out fast!" he said. "The gun is going to explode!"

Although Paul knew that his father's physical body was several thousand miles away in China Point, he was not at all confounded by his appearance in the soul body. Paul leaped over the side of the gun tub, shouting at his crew to get out fast.

The last of the crew had just made it to the deck, about ten feet below the gun tub, when the gun blew up.

Later when Paul was home on a furlough, he asked his father about this incident, but Pop only smiled. He never spoke about the experience, but they both knew what had happened that day.

Another most interesting incident occurred when Paul's ship was just off San Francisco on its way back to the States. According to Twitchell, he was lying on his bunk one evening, half-asleep, when he began to wander around in his soul body.

"When one is frightened and in danger of his life, he is apt to have his spiritual senses open," Paul remarked. "That is why I must have been pulled back to Guam, where, on the north end of the island, one of our young troopers had got himself lost outside of the lines and had wandered into the jungle and cave area where there were Japanese guerrillas still in hiding."

"Hey, buddy," Twitchell said, appearing beside the marine, "want a lift back to the lines?"

The trooper wheeled, his rifle at the ready. "Where did you come from, sailor?"

"Never mind that now," Paul told him. "The important thing is that I know where the American

55

lines are. Are you going to follow me or stay out here and listen to the night birds screech at each other?"

Paul disappeared soon after he had led the marine to safety, but some mutual friends heard the trooper describing the Navy man who had rescued him and spoke up that he sounded an awfully lot like Paul Twitchell.

"I was asked about this later," Paul told me, "but I would never admit it. It would only have caused a great deal of skepticism and ridicule, so it was best to keep quiet."

There was one time when the young sailor who could be in two places at once did not heed his own counsel, however.

"Boy, I'm glad we'll be going to the Philippines for a change," Paul remarked as the port captain came on deck for final inspection before the ship sailed out of San Francisco.

The port captain gave the young seaman a startled look, then hurried to the bridge. Paul knew, with a terrible sinking feeling inside his skull, that he had made that much-warned-against "slip of the lip." Whenever a ship sailed from port, the captain himself would not open his sealed orders and read the destination until the vessel was several miles from harbor. Prior to the moment when the ship's captain opened his orders, only the port captain knew the destination of the ship. It was wartime, and such security precautions were necessary to prevent enemy intelligence from learning U.S. patterns of troop dispersal and shipping routes.

But now, to the port captain's alarm, a young gunnery officer had just told him where the ship was headed!

"Pretty soon I was surrounded by security officers and taken to the bridge," Paul said. "I had seen our orders via the ECK-Vidya method of seeing the future, but I managed to beg out of the situation by saying that I had just made a lucky guess. For a few uncomfortable moments, I thought it was going to be arrest and court martial for me, but then they decided that I couldn't really have known and they tried to pass the whole incident off."

Paul lay on his bunk that night and made a vow that he would put a hobble on that tongue of his. It was not yet time for him to declare the message of Eckankar.

4. From Cliff-Hanger to Spiritual Adept

For this book, I asked Paul Twitchell to describe his spiritual growth leading to his work in Eckankar.

"Well, Paul, those readers who have followed us this far into the book have come to know you as a remarkably complex person. I suppose the question that is foremost in their minds, as it was in mine, is how the sensitive little boy from China Point, who had, by way of understatement, a most unusual childhood, became the spiritual leader that he is today. Then, too, there is the added complexity of your metamorphosis into the soul-traveling 'Little Toughie.' From Navy gunner to guru is quite a step."

"It gets even more complicated, Brad. For quite a while there, I was a full-fledged Cliff-Hanger."

"Perhaps you should explain just what a Cliff-Hanger is."

"Indeed I must, for the reader needs to understand that after the Second World War, I underwent a very confused period of spiritual struggle as I sought to co-exist with contemporary American culture.

"At that time, nothing in this century made sense to me. I seemed to be a man born out of his time, and for that reason I was not interested in the ordinary man's grubbing for money. I could see that this era in our history was honoring mediocrity until it was fast becoming the stabilizing force of society. I could see our machine age developing an educational system which would produce tame rabbits and robots for the politicians to manage. I wanted to turn away from the claptrap of this supermarket culture, which was placing so much emphasis upon so-called 'aids for better living.' I wanted to seek the same purpose in life that had driven St. Anthony of the Desert, Jacob Bohme, and St. John of the Cross. I sought that goal which we call the transcendental consciousness.

"The Cliff-Hanger tag was coined to explain my attitude regarding this age of mass culture. The name itself summons an image of a man who hangs on the edge of the cliffs of Nirvana—safe from the crowd, more outside than Colin Wilson's *Outsider*, happier than the angry young men of England, and at the very opposite pole from Jean Paul Sartre's existentialism with its claim that man has no hope.

"As a Cliff-Hanger, I did a lot of crazy things. I took to wearing sport caps, mainly just to create a little stir at the newspapers where I worked. In protest to the 'seal of approval' a certain women's magazine goes around slapping on things, I had an artist draw a picture of me with my sport cap and my fingers curled in an 'OK' sign of approval and went around giving out my own 'Recommended by Paul Twitchell' awards.

"If I liked any of the several thousand books a year I used to check out of libraries around the country, I would give them my 'Paul Twitchell Good Reading Award.' If they didn't meet my standards, they would get the 'Sour Grapes Award.'"

"This seems to have been your social protest period, Paul."

"Indeed it was, Brad. I was definitely searching and trying to give full meaning to my life.

"I suppose this protest period grew out of the fact that, shortly after the war, I had returned to see Sudar Singh in Allahabad. It was while renewing my physical bonds with Sudar Singh that I met the ancient Tibetan master, Rebazar Tarzs, who is said to be several hundred years old. It was under this holy man that I truly began to perfect my study of Eckankar and to master the techniques of soul travel, the ancient path to God-consciousness."

"Didn't your controversial book, The Tiger's Fang, *come out of this meeting with Rebazar Tarzs?"*

"Basically, yes."

"Could you tell us something about the content of this book and about the storm of controversy which it has raised?"

"The book itself deals with a spiritual journey through each of the many heavens. Each of these spiritual planes is under the aegis of a different deity, and the book is primarily composed of dialogues with these entities. Some of the chapter titles are 'The Spiritual Fallacy,' 'The Secret Teachings,' 'Man and Woman,' 'The Hideous God of Life,' 'The Spiritual Malignancy,' 'Saviours in Limbo,' 'Fierce Children of Light,' 'The Worship of Moloch.' "

"Sounds intriguing, and I know it is, because I've read The Tiger's Fang. *Why the controversy, Paul?"*

"The controversy was not unexpected, Brad. In my introduction to the book, I said that the material found in *The Tiger's Fang* would shake the foundation of the teachings of orthodox religions, philosophies, and metaphysical concepts. I also stated that I knew the book would create many diverse points of view, namely curiosity, inspiration, and antagonism, and I emphasized that the book, if read with an open mind, would open up new spiritual vistas for the reader.

"I have been told by friends who are clergymen in the Roman Catholic Church that their institution is almost completely divided in their reaction to the book. I have even heard that the Pope himself has read the book and was greatly disturbed by it, perhaps to the point of condemning it.

"One of my *chelas* sent a copy of the book to her son stationed in Saigon. The Army censors got hold of it and became very confused. They couldn't decide what it was all about, so they called in the lad, who was on a sensitive job, and asked him who Paul Twitchell was.

"He told them I was a 'friend' of his mother's. Then they asked him what I meant by certain statements in the book. He said that he could offer no opinion, as they had taken the book before he had had a chance to read it. They wanted to know why I would write a book of such a nature and just what I was up to. The lad could only reply that the only fact he could attest to was that I was acquainted with his mother and that I had written the book in question.

"He was taken off his job for ten days while the censor perused the book to see if it met with their non-political requirements. After this period, they handed him *The Tiger's Fang* and put him back on the job."

"So the Army censors must have approved The Tiger's Fang?"

"Whether they approved of it or not, I don't know, at least they surely gave it a careful reading. Maybe it even did them some good."

"Have you heard how such a figure as the Maharishi Mahesh Yogi reacts to your book?"

"I have been told by several people, who have reported his statements back to me, that he has said that I am the only person he knows who can write a book like *The Tiger's Fang* and not live in a cave in the Himalayas.

"Someone asked him in Toronto if there were anyone he knew who had ever developed the God-state of consciousness and still been able to continue as much as possible in the physical body. His answer was: 'There is one man in the United

States who does. His name is Paul Twitchell, and his book *The Tiger's Fang* proves that he is able to do this.'

"On another occasion, when he was asked if anyone had ever surpassed the method that he is teaching, the Maharishi Mahesh Yogi is said to have replied: 'Only one person that I know. He has reached the true God-realm. He is that American who wrote *The Tiger's Fang*.'

"Such statements from the Maharishi have sold a lot of copies of my book!"

"Did you begin teaching Eckankar upon your return to the States?"

"No, my brain was literally on fire with all the spiritual truths that it had assimilated under the tutelage of Rebazar Tarzs. It was impossible for me to return to the United States and accept conventional employment, and yet I was unsure of myself, unable to decide whether or not I was strong enough to carry the message of something as weighty as Eckankar to the West."

"We're talking about pre-Cliff-Hanger days now, aren't we?"

"Well, I've always been a Cliff-Hanger, I guess; but, yes, this was before I took roots on the West Coast in the late 1950's."

"What did you do in this period of—if you'll excuse the expression—soul searching?"

"Some crazy, wild things, I'm afraid."

"For instance."

"Well, this for instance. I met up with some wild Australians who believed that they could find a fortune in gold in New Guinea. After talking with them one night, I projected myself and explored the area in my *Atma Sarup*. They were right. There was gold in the rivers and mountains where they had heard that the precious metal existed. While in the soul body, I even spotted a good lode in the Owen

Stanley Range beyond Port Moresby.

"The expedition was poorly equipped, and I had little faith in the possibility of our ragtag crew being able to actually get any gold out of the area; but I went along anyway for the adventure.

"We really did find some gold, but we also found a tribe of Bushmen who began to pursue us. I think it was more a child's game on their part, but they looked too fierce to play with. They chased us out of the area, but I really doubt if they would have done more than frighten the wits out of us if they had caught us. We turned our small booty over to a government office, and we were given a small pile of money for our trouble. We were advised to take the first boat back to Australia, and we happily did so."

"I know that during this period in your life you also did such things as diving for pearls off La Paz, Mexico, and investigating Voodoo in Haiti. When did you really begin to settle down and start to formulate a serious manner in which you might spread the message of Eckankar?"

"Probably when my sister, Kay-Dee, died in 1959. She had told me several months before her death that she would soon die. Kay-Dee apparently knew when her time had come, for she went into her room during the late afternoon and lay down on the bed. She was called for dinner, and when there was no answer, her body was discovered. The doctors termed it a natural death, but Kay-Dee had just known when her life had run out.

"My father died of cancer at about the same time, but he was not in his body for many months before his death. I visited him once a few weeks before his passing. He was lying on the bed with his eyes closed. I knew he was out of the body, so I said, 'Pop, you're not fooling me. You're not here.' He opened his eyes, winked slowly at me, and said nothing."

"It was then that you became a Cliff-Hanger in earnest."

"Correct. I was in full rebellion against the conformity of this weird society that we live in. I pulled a lot of wild capers and wore my goofy sports caps to purposely upset many a solid authority and stuffed-shirt.

"I also began to write short stories under a half-a-dozen *noms-de-plume* in order to be able to keep my independence and freedom. I was holding down various newspaper jobs off and on in the Seattle area, but I would spend several hours each night in my daily writing stint, with a cap perched on my head, both feet cocked under me in yoga fashion, and sometimes a bottle of iced champagne beside my chair.

"In my best writing year I sold some two hundred short stories and articles, and, altogether, I published a half-dozen novels and books."

"When did the Cliff-Hanger begin his transformation into spiritual adept?"

"The switchover from the Cliff-Hanger to ECK began taking place after I met my present wife, Gail. She insisted that I do something with my knowledge and abilities.

"We were married in 1964 in San Francisco, and shortly afterwards Rebazar Tarzs began to appear and give me intensive instructions. He had been appearing regularly in the latter fifties, but he said that those sessions had only been designed to prepare me for the exhaustive drills which now faced me. I was told to move south, to choose San Diego for our home.

"One day Gail and I were strolling around San Francisco's Chinatown, and we wandered into an old Chinese temple. There a priest told me that I would be moving to San Diego soon and would start my life's work in ECK.

"Shortly after our move, I requested some lecture time at the California Parapsychology Foundation, and I gave six months of lectures.

"I used to walk the beach at night, wondering if I could take the responsibility, but gradually, this task has become more and more acceptable, until now I gladly carry the full burden.

"My first out-of-town lecture was at Long Beach, where three gentle ladies, two widows and a spinster, came. I decided that I could lecture as well to three as to three hundred. Word began to get around about ECK, so I agreed to write the monthly discourses and to offer instruction by mail. I went from three *chelas* to thousands in less than three years."

"Tell us about Gail. It sounds as though she might have been the catalyst that gave the Eckankar movement its greatest boost."

"Gail is twenty-five, but she looks eighteen. She has now gone back to college and is majoring in psychology. We met in the Seattle Public Library in 1963. She had a part-time job there while she attended the University of Washington as a full-time student. I was reading a tremendous amount of books at the time. I would take out twenty books each evening and I would trade them in for a fresh batch on the next night.

"Gail had been puzzling about this unusual fellow who left his crazy bookmarks in the returned books, and she had been wanting to know more about him. One evening she was on the checkout and return desk, and I approached her with an armload of books. 'Oh,' she said, 'so you're Mr. Twitchell.'

"That started the romance. Our courtship period was quite unique, however. I went right to work to educate her in ECK, and every day for two years I wrote her a two-page letter on Eckankar. Not a word of love or romance was given in these letters, but every sentence dealt with Eckankar, from the beginning of the teachings to the higher level.

"I wouldn't marry Gail until she turned twenty-one. I wanted her to understand that our marriage would be for keeps. She persisted and I persisted. I went to San Francisco in late November of '64 and left her in Seattle. Then I couldn't stand it there without her, so I drove back to her home near South Bend, Washington, and married her.

"The first year was rough, but we made it. She worked and I wrote discourses on Eckankar. The next year we moved from San Francisco to San Diego, where Gail went to work in a small city library. Gail now believed that it was time for me to bring out ECK, just as the ECK masters had been telling me. I had promised Gail that she might go back to college and complete her education when I went to ECK full-time, so she is a student once again."

"Paul, how widespread is Eckankar at the present time?"

"The headquarters for ECK is presently in Las Vegas, although we hope to establish a worldwide center for the movement in Srinagar, Kashmir, within a few more years. Currently we have our European headquarters in Zurich, Switzerland, and a Pacific office at Aukland. We have group study centers throughout the world, with twenty-five study groups here in the States."

"From all reports that I have heard, your 1967 lecture tour of Europe was a great success. I know that you met with such notables as editor Peter Carvel; Harry Edwards, the spiritual healer; Croiset, the Dutch psychic; Dr. Hans Wyss, Swiss publisher of spiritual books; Dr. Hans Naegeli, noted Zurich psychiatrist; Dr. Schaefer-Schulmeyer, Director of the Bad Prymont sanitorium in Germany; Dora Bryan, English musical star; and many others. What, however, impressed you most during your European tour?"

"The thing that impressed me most, Brad, was the enormous hunger for God among the masses of adults. Directly opposite this was the decline and fall of spiritual values among the youth in a society that fails to establish a clear definition of the higher ethics of religion and right living.

"These positive and negative values clash not only in Europe, of course, but in every part of the world today. There is a lack of true spiritual teachings throughout the world.

"Adults are not getting satisfaction from their religious faiths, and youth is being misguided by negative values. Too many leaders are telling our youth that they can have freedom through drugs and harmful ideologies—none of which have any essence of God contained within them."

"I also learned that you took time out from your lectures to exorcise, or 'dehaunt,' a house in Scotland."

"Brad, I am constantly asked to do this sort of thing, and while it is true that I have exorcised quite a number of homes, it is not too much of a regular thing on my agenda. In fact it's a little boring in a sense, and I refuse a large number of requests to go poking about in old houses."

"Could you indulge me with the details, Paul? You know that I am interested in such phenomena."

"Surely. I did this strictly as a favor for a friend. The ghost had become something of a nuisance in his old home about fifty miles southeast of Edinburgh. The ghost was that of a member of a gang of rogues that had been hanged by Sir George Homes during the reign of James VI. He had fallen victim to Jeddart justice, which hanged a man first and tried him afterwards. Anyway, this poor ghost had been sticking around since the seventeenth century, haunting its former home. Few people had been able to live there, and my friend was about to give the residence up as a lost cause. So on my trip to Scotland this past summer, I saw what could be done for the old spirit. In a short time, I sent him away to rest in the summerland of the astral world."

"Thanks for the indulgence! Paul, have you ever used out-of-body travel to help find missing persons or to track down criminals?"

"Yes, I have on occasion participated in such activities. One case I remember in particular occurred in Baltimore. The son of socially prominent parents had been missing for quite some time and could not be traced by the proper authorities. The young man was about twenty-four, and, though not wild, he was a bit inclined to lead an active nightlife. No expense or effort had been spared, but the official search had been completely fruitless.

"I projected myself out of the body, searched for him, and soon found his body. He was at the bottom of the bay, weighted down with iron rails. The police got a diving company to search for him, and they brought him out of the water for proper burial."

"Did you receive proper recognition for having been the one to locate the body?"

"Oh, no, indeed not! Such a thing would never happen. At least not yet. You won't find many police or other official and government bureaus who will admit that they use people with 'special' talents in their investigations.

"Along the same line I might mention that many of the trips I take out of the country are for a very definite reason. I meet and talk with many officials of various governments. Such meetings are always held in the strictest of secrecy, and security measures are most rigidly enforced. These officials do not want anyone to know that they would consult with one like myself in matters of state.

"There have been moments of danger in doing such things as these, and once I was at the point of being kidnapped. Only the vigilance of the security people of that country saved me.

"I never get any open financial remuneration for

any of this sort of thing. Every now and then, however, someone will see that I get so much payment; but it is always in cash, of course, and there is never any way by which the money can be traced to the payee."

"Now that you've brought up money, Paul, I feel compelled to say that some chelas *have been more than a little disappointed by various gurus who are quite obviously lining their own pockets with the high fees which they demand for exercises in consciousness expansion and the like. We both know that one very highly touted Indian savant has a Swiss bank account against his old age, and that many other gurus of both high and low rank are piling up their own private Fort Knoxes under the guise of religion. Would you care to comment just how Eckankar is run financially? I don't mean to offend you by bringing this up."*

"Not at all, Brad. In fact I am happy to answer this question.

"I do not run Eckankar as a non-profit organization. Most people in this line of work do indeed use the religious non-profit organization provision as an escape clause on their taxes. Eckankar is licensed in the state of Nevada as a business organization. I do this because I feel that it is only proper and fitting that I make my own way instead of trying to get under a tax shelter. It is hard, of course, but I manage to do it.

"Now I am not trying to come off as an ultra-patriot, but this is my country, and I want to help support it by paying my share of the load.

"Nor am I trying to sound pretentious when I say that I do not feel that it is honest to ask the public to support me in a foundation which would be free of taxes. But I believe that if the man on the street must pay his taxes, there is no reason why I should try to get out of paying mine.

"There is too much dishonesty among those who try to get tax shelters because they claim to be religious groups. God didn't establish non-taxable foundations, so why should I try to get under such claims?

"If ECK cannot take care of itself, then it can be of little value to anyone else!"

5.   Conversations
with Rebazar Tarzs

While Paul Twitchell was undergoing the transition
from Cliff-Hanger to spiritual adept, the Tibetan
master of Eckankar, Rebazar Tarzs, appeared in the
soul body to administer a series of lessons to Paulji in
his home in Seattle, Washington. In this chapter, Sri
Paul Twitchell has consented to share some of the
wisdom of those talks with the spiritual traveler.

"In the state of consciousness of the individual is
to be found the explanation of the phenomena of
life. If man's concept of himself were different,
everything in his world would be different. His
concept of himself being what it is, everything in his
world must be as it is. This is the doctrine of
Eckankar. Is it clear?"

Twitchell said, "It is clearly explained. But I want
to know something else. Why aren't the people of this
world being told the truth today? Why must
everything be hidden behind ritual and mystery?"

Rebazar Tarzs replied, "God is an unconditional
force, available to every man, but to let every man
know this would be dangerous in the world of time
and space. So those in charge of the welfare of the
human race will care for man until he is ready to take
care of himself and to use this force on a universal
basis.

"Let us put it this way. Facts are nothing but
symbols of the inner self that *homo sapiens* does not
understand, but which are easily grasped by *homo*

immortalis. Science and medicine are scandalously overrated systems for misinterpreting ascertained facts. Nine-tenths of all religious organizations intend to keep their people mystified, because mystery holds loyalty.

"Man is unaware of how much hypnotism and clairvoyance is used in secret police work on the international fronts. Russia uses it in her spy work, and so do America and England. But if you were to suggest this to the average man, he would laugh at you as if you were crazy. For this reason such knowledge is well hidden. You became aware of how the natives in the country of India are able to leave their bodies almost at will to explore other worlds and areas, then come back to their bodies. You have seen how criminals are caught through this method or by clairvoyance. Hypnotism has been used in India for thousands of years in such a common way that nobody even thinks of it as paranormal.

"One must come to realize that all creation is finished in the lower universes. Creativeness is only a deeper receptiveness, for the entire contents of all time and all space, while experienced in a time sequence, actually coexist in an infinite and eternal NOW. In fact, all that mankind ever was, or ever will be in these lower worlds, exists NOW! This is what is meant by creation. The statement that creation is finished means that nothing is ever to be created, it is only manifested. What is called creativity is only that process of becoming aware of what already IS. You simply become aware of increasing portions of that which already exists. The fact that you can never be anything that you are not already or experience anything that does not already exist explains the whole of creation existing in you, and it is your destiny to become increasingly aware of its infinite wonders and to experience even greater and greater portions of it.

"In short, it appears that events change, but what really happens is that we shift our viewpoint from event to event, even though the event is stationary and fixed. That is what I mean when I say that all creation is finished. All events, all situations, and all forms are co-existing and make themselves known in our lives as we view them. It is the recognition of them which is important, the awakening of man. Man does not evolve, he awakens. He moves in his assumptions of his own limited consciousness."

"You see the great religions of the world, however different in their detailed doctrines, spring from one and the same source—the universal religious consciousness of mankind, the universal impulsation of one and the same mystical being.

"Understand this: The God we know is like a great whirling vortex, out of which comes spirit. This spirit is like a sea, and man is a fish swimming in this sea. This is what we might call the ocean of love and mercy.

"When the mind of man is illuminated, he becomes a part of God, the realization of the absolute. Illumination comes through waiting upon the Lord, that is, by resting in the consciousness of the omnipresence. It is not through struggle, effort, supplication, or merit. No one except those who are traveling the path of ECK can determine when it occurs."

Twitchell asked, "What type of mind grasps the illuminated state best?"

Rebazar Tarzs replied, "A mind with randomity. That is, a mind which can change under any circumstance. The higher a soul travels the spiritual path, the less its burdens become, and the easier it is to change swiftly from one course to another. A mind that moves with random speed works in the field of randomity."

"God never established an exclusive group for the liberation of man. He has given the power to many for the particular way back to his kingdom. There are certain paths that one must follow, some better than others, because the masters of these particular ways have developed the resources for their *chelas* in seeking the way. This is because men are at all sorts of levels of consciousness and not all can follow one universal way."

"Each man's world is a solid thought or materialized mindstuff. The idea is to bring into expression the good and beautiful. This is done by getting the good and beautiful properly arranged in the consciousness."

"So we come to the most important part of life's message. It is not what we do that determines our experience in life, but it is what we expect. Even if you have done all the correct things, and still maintain the haunting fear that things will go wrong, they will go wrong. Is it because you are bad, sinful, or evil? No. It is because you have the belief.

"Now you are coming into the level of understanding wherein we cease trying to demonstrate things but, rather, move into a greater expression and find that the things we need are already supplied. We demonstrate the giver and not the gift: we demonstrate God and not the things of God."

"Saints, devils, and credulous fools are made of the same identical stuff. They all have visions. They see the same truth from different aspects. Devils exploit stupidity. They create blinding fear that gives them power over others. Such fear inflates the devils' feeling of importance, and it makes the fools think that the devils are the only safe leaders to follow. But the visions of the saints—like prisms letting light into darkness—diffuses the material fog, the fog that blinds the best of men and makes men victims of want, disease, and crime. The visions of the saints let in affluence and magnanimity and vigor. Naturally, the devils hate this. If they can't pervert the saint's vision to their own ends, they try to destroy it."

"One of the most prevalent misunderstandings is that the law of God works only for those who have a devout or religious objective. This is a fallacy. It works just as impersonally as the law of electricity works. It can be used for greed or selfish purposes as well as for noble tasks. But it should always be borne in mind that ignoble thoughts and actions inevitably result in unhappy consequences."

"The secret of harmonious love is the development of the spiritual consciousness, as any spiritual traveler will tell us. In this consciousness, fear and anxiety disappear and life becomes meaningful, with fulfillment as its keynote. The individual becomes a dweller in the higher consciousness.

"This has been one of the differences that ECK makes with established religion. The authorities put a great deal of emphasis on rituals, moral codes, and laws, but seldom do they speak about rising above good and evil, or love and hate, or polarizing upon the dichotomy of good. This is one of the most subtle points of all life. Remember James 1:8, "A double-minded man is unstable in all his ways."

"The power of attention is the measure of the inner force. Concentrated observation of one thing shuts out other things and causes them to disappear. The great secret of being spiritually minded is to focus the attention of the feeling of spirituality without permitting any distraction. All progress depends on the increase in the attention span of time.

The ideas which impel you to action are those which dominate the consciousness, those which possess the attention.

"To the unenlightened this will seem to be all fantasy, yet progress comes from those who do not take accepted views nor accept the world as it is. When we set out to master the movement of attention, which must be done if we would successfully alter the course of observed events, it is then we realize how little control we exercise over the mind and how much it is dominated by sensory impressions and by being set adrift on tides of other men's considerations and environmental moods.

"A tense person is wrapped up in himself, his immediate family, the events of his past, the prospects of his future, or how he is regarded by other people.

"What does this tension do? It grips. It causes a stranglehold on the channels within him. It cuts off thinking. It is useless for such a person to relax physically as long as he continues to center the mind upon himself. The stranglehold will be there every minute, day and night. When we learn to love others as ourselves, the attention will be focused outwardly, and therefore we will become relaxed. There will be no stranglehold within and the mind will become free."

"God gave us dominion through consciousness, and this consciousness, which is the creative principle of our body, must also be its sustaining and maintaining principle.

"Once you have this principle, you have caught the entire principle of life. Literally, this is the law of life—the substance, the activity, the intelligent direction of life which is within man as well as outside.

"We only have to prove this in some one direction

and we shall have it proved in every direction. The whole secret lies in the word 'heart' or what we call consciousness. An intellectual knowledge of the fact that God is all is of no value. The only value any truth has is in the degree of its realization. Truth realized via ECK is spiritual consciousness. If we are conscious of the presence of the Lord, if we are conscious of the activity of God, then so it is unto us."

"Self-examination is one of the worst things a person can do. Hundreds of thousands of persons damn themselves daily by indulging in self-analysis. They are like fools taking a radio apart to discover why a program annoys them.

"Self-analysis without experienced guidance is worse than taking patent medicine to cure an undiagnosed ailment. Much worse, in fact. A wrong diagnosis is sometimes a sentence to death. Self-conviction of sin is always a sentence to hell. Always. There is no exception to this. Man is hampered by conventional education, conservative theories, public prejudice, self-ignorance, and much too much familiarity with evidence that seems to prove the contrary to what intuition shows man is true.

"It makes no difference what a man becomes. Greater men than the bishops of the churches have become beggars, not cardinals. Nevertheless, one can become great in God and save many a poor wretch from hopelessness.

"Now remember this: As the great spiritual guru Yaubl Sacabi once said, 'Knowledge is one thing, virtue is another.' Philosophy, no matter how enlightening it may be, gives no command over the passions, no influential motives, no inescapable principles. It is not worth much in the crises of mankind. How can it help in time of epidemics?"

"True happiness is a sensation of momentary balance. When man remembers who, and what, he really is, he does no wrong and injures no one. Even his worst mistakes turn out to help others; and they become profitable lessons for all."

"Gradually, as man struggles toward God, the illusion of this life loses its hypnotic grip. We begin to be free to think clearly and to solve problems sanely. We leave off trying to fill holes with shadows. Instead, we try to fill them with ideas that develop their own substance. So it follows that anyone seeing on a spiritual plane, but working for material personal profit, is committing spiritual treason. This is why spies and criminals who use clairvoyance, as many of them consciously do, invariably meet disaster. Clairvoyance perverted to treacherous ends becomes spiritual suicide. Sometimes it leads one into the madhouse. It is always, without any exception, without any possible exception, ruinous to the one who misuses it."

"Let it be known here and now that all knowledge and all wisdom is never given to a soul. For the world of God is without beginning and without ending, infinite in all attributes and qualities, and constantly expanding toward the greater truth and greater wisdom."

"If one prays for an object, or a desire, verily, it shall come unto him because his mind shall create what he desires. But the true consciousness should never be blinded by that which the intellect devises.

"When anyone prays to get something, he is praying in reality to have his reality in this world acted upon. And if he prays to have his senses acted upon by an outer source, then how will this bring one any true spirituality?

"Act, rather, that we might give mastership qualities which are already within us. As we unfold constantly to give, we are not unfolding to have our senses acted upon. We are unfolding to give all that we and our senses are capable of giving. Then shall our lives be transformed.

"And in the transformation, we shall realize all of the capabilities, all of the gifts, all of the demonstrations of life which are radiated by those in the spiritual worlds."

"Spirituality is not attained by denying the world, nor by affirming the spiritual world. Spirituality *is*, because there has never been a time in the world, in the true world, where God, or spirituality, was not."

"Illusions are like mistresses. We can have many of them without tying ourselves down to responsibility. But truth insists on marriage. Once a person embraces truth, he is in its ruthless, but gentle, grasp."

"God is love; God is life; God is spirit; God is all. That is true whether we are saints or sinners. It is true whether we are young or old, Jew, Gentile, Oriental, or Occidental, regardless of creed or color. There is no way in which God can be left out of His own universe, nor can we leave ourselves out of it.

"God is; there is always a God. This God is infinite in nature, eternal, universal, impersonal, impartial, and omnipresent. But how do we avail ourselves of that which the *Sugmad* is? How do we bring God into our individual experience? We must know and practice the principle of the heavenly kingdom until we become proficient in its application. It must be in our God experience. God is and God is here and God is now. But God is available only in proportion to our realization and willingness to accept the discipline that is necessary for the attainment of that selfhood we call God-realization.

"We must say to ourselves, to God: Show us what we must do in order to avail ourselves of this principle, this life, this love, and to live the life of soul. When we have reached this state of readiness, we have begun to travel the path which leads to spiritual consciousness."

"Unless we feel the actual presence of God, then, as far as we are concerned, we do not have realization of this Spirit. It is like electricity, which is everywhere, just as the Spirit of God is, but electricity is of little use or value to anyone unless it is connected in some way for his particular use. So it is with the Spirit of God. It is everywhere in an absolute, spiritual sense, but it is only effective in our experience to the extent to which It is realized."

"It is possible for anyone to change the trend of his life, not by hearing or reading truth, but by making it an active part of his consciousness in daily experience, until it becomes a habit every moment of the day, instead of an occasional thought. Let God operate in the consciousness morning, noon, and night, until gradually the actual awareness comes. Then we make the transition from being hearers of the word to being doers of the word. Then we shall be living in the world and shall gather in the harvest of souls."

6.   *Traveling in the Soul Body*

One night, as Paul Twitchell was entering the auditorium of the California Parapsychology Foundation, a woman approached him in great excitement. "I have just had my first out-of-the-body experience," she said.

Twitchell was at the time conducting a workshop in bilocation, and he was pleased with his student's success. He could see, however, that the woman was a bit apprehensive and wished to talk about her experience. No other students had yet entered the auditorium, so Paulji sat and indicated that he would be pleased to hear the details of the woman's accomplishment.

"I was sitting in meditation last night," she began, "and I was doing exactly what you told me to do. Then I heard this funny noise which sounded like the popping of a cork from a bottle, and I found myself standing on the other side of the room looking at my body in the chair!"

Paul Twitchell knew that his *chela* had experienced that spiritual phenomenon which is rather common to those people who become serious students of supernatural reality. Long ago he had learned that a careful study of the lives of the Christian saints and the Eastern adepts would indicate that such phenomena are living experiences which can be brought under the control of the operator himself. Bilocation, or astral projection as it is more frequently termed, is, in Sri Paul Twitchell's opinion, a manifestation of the lower planes.

"When I was a kid playing around with slipping in and out of the body, I was projecting myself in the

81

astral body, the *Nuri Sarup*. Kay-Dee and I would play all sorts of games in our 'light bodies,' as the Hindus call them. We would leap out of windows in our *Nuri Sarup* bodies, bob above the roof of the house, and pester the animals around our home. Mom, of course, would put her foot down on such tomfoolery, and she would often take the whip to us. This may not have been a bad idea; for at that time, we had no sense of adult morality, which must be a part of the *modus operandi* of bilocation."

It was during the year with Sudar Singh that Paulji and Kay-Dee learned to travel in their soul bodies, their *Atma Sarups*.

"The *Atma Sarup*, the soul body, travels beyond the astral plane to the higher levels where the true teachings are found in their entirety. The astral body is limited to the first interplane.

"Sudar Singh would open the consciousness of his *chelas*—provided they were ready—and allow the light of spirit to flow through them. Many of the students were too busy with their self-made troubles to see what he was doing; because of this, perhaps, Sudar Singh did some of his most effective teaching in the dream state.

"He would come to each of us while we were asleep," Twitchell said, "and take us out in our *Atma Sarup* to some far corner of the inner planes where he would give us instruction in Eckankar, the ancient science of soul travel."

In the February 1967 issue of *The New Cosmic Star*, Paulji told that publication's readers how they might acquire "Out-of-Body Teachings via the Dream State."

"The way of doing this is very simple," Twitchell instructs. "Trust in a teacher to take care of your inner life until you are able to be on your own; then it is likely you will have the experience of learning by dreams as I did."

A spiritual teacher, according to Twitchell, will take the *chela* out nightly into the other worlds to be taught on different planes. "You meet in the first of the light worlds with a teacher whose *Atma Sarup* is stationed there to link up with you (the *chela*) in your light body and take you to some respective point in the spirit land to explore or study.

"However, one can do some of this on his own, if he does not have a teacher who works with him, in this manner. Lie down at night and count yourself into sleep. That is, make a postulate that you are going to be asleep by a certain number, e.g. ten or fifteen. Following this you will know that you are going to 'be out' by the time that your physical self falls into a sleep.

"Generally you will make the count and drop off to sleep. But almost at once you are awake in the light body standing off in a corner of the room looking at your physical body asleep on the bed. Then you take off for another plane in hope of finding something that is worth this trouble of traveling in the light body.

"You will generally return before morning unless something disturbs your body upon the bed. Often there is a division of consciousness that gives one a dual impression of being both in the physical and in the light body. This dual consciousness is not unusual when practicing the dream technique of inner traveling.

"However, you will usually be with a teacher or guide on the inside world, for your progress is always watched, so as not to hit any psychic snarls along the way. If allowed, your teacher will make suggestions and steer you in certain directions so that you will get the greatest benefit from these journeys."

Can man really project his astral self to faraway places? A number of leading psychologists have recently declared that certain specially gifted people are able to separate their minds from their bodies. These investigators have amassed case studies which tell of men and women who have projected themselves to cities thousands of miles from their homes to appear mysteriously before friends and relatives or to drift spiritlike in an atmosphere free of time, space, or physical barriers.

Dr. Eugene E. Bernard, a North Carolina State University psychologist, is currently doing research on the phenomenon of out-of-the-body experience. "I believe that man has the ability to perform this feat," Dr. Bernard has told newsmen. "If he can be taught to project the control, the prospects are staggering. These experiences are definitely not hallucinations."

Dr. Gardiner Murphy, director of research for the Menninger Foundation, has expressed his opinion that ". . . out-of-body experiences appear to be real."

In 1952, Dr. Hornel Hart submitted a questionnaire to 155 students at Duke University, which asked the question: "Have you ever actually seen your physical body from a viewpoint completely outside that body, like standing beside the bed and looking at yourself lying in bed, or floating in the air near your body?"

Thirty per cent of the students queried answered *Yes.* After studying several other student groups, Dr. Hart concluded that at least 20% of college-level young people believe that they have experienced some form of astral projection.

Researcher Frederic W.H. Myers has written that cases of astral projection present ". . . the most extraordinary achievement of the human will. What can lie further outside any known capacity than the power to cause a semblance of oneself to appear at a distance? What can be more in a central action—more manifestly the outcome of whatsoever is deepest and most unitary in man's whole being? Of all vital phenomena, I say, this is the most significant; this self-projection is the one definite act which it seems as though a man might perform equally well before and after bodily death."

Since his year with Sudar Singh, Paul Twitchell has studied every feasible out-of-body theory known. He has made subsequent trips abroad to the Orient where he has read manuscripts, talked with adepts, gurus, and holy men on the subject of soul projection. For purposes of comparison with Eckankar, Paulji has also practiced all the techniques.

Twitchell claims that many of the students who attended his Eckankar workshops at the California Parapsychology Foundation were able to have at least some degree of success in controlling out-of-the-body experiences. Paulji also maintains that he has perfected the techniques of soul travel to the point where he can teach them via the mails. At my request, he again gave me full access to his files on those *chelas* who have developed a certain amount of prowess at slipping in and out of their bodies.

A Mr. M.R. from South Carolina wrote in November of 1967 to report that he was making progress in his lessons: "I had a wonderful experience this morning at about 6:30. I couldn't sleep a bit last night, and as I was lying there, I sank into a semiconscious state, and my spirit would almost leave my body. It seems my spirit from the neck down would rise, then it would fall back into my body. I could actually feel it when it fell back. It was just like raising my leg and letting it fall back down on the bed. It was a wonderful feeling."

Mr. M.R. is but a neophyte, of course; but a letter from Mr. C.C. of San Francisco indicates a *chela* well on his way to mastering soul travel, as taught in the Eckankar doctrines.

"I'm finding much better awareness and control

when working from the soul planes. My practice now is to begin observing each of the bodies and working up to the soul plane. Each time I do this they are much easier to discern. Of course, I then attempt to see how they interrelate. And I find that a very subtle shift of identity is taking place. I am less body, personality, C.C., etc. and more real self.

"My most recent development: Consciousness does not seem necessarily 'tied down' to any particular one of the bodies. Last night, after I had gone to bed, I found myself seemingly going to sleep while simultaneously shifting my consciousness to another state. This is actually a common experience for me, but each time that it has happened, I've been startled by it and promptly wake up with a jolt. Last night I became fascinated with the phenomenon and tried to control it. I think I managed some control. I remember feeling quite astonished at how unattached to the body I seemed to be."

A Mrs. N.C. has also progressed quite far along the path of Eckankar, for according to her letter: ". . . I am progressing with my out-of-the-body experiences. Last night I felt myself leave my body and look back on it as I walked upstairs.

"My oldest son is having out-of-the-body experiences. He told me of a fire he witnessed in which two dogs suffocated. Within a few days, the incident was recorded in our local paper."

Mr. W.C.T. of Chicago describes an experience which occurred to him while he was in deep meditation. ". . . I suddenly felt that I was a mist or a light breeze that moved from the bedroom into the front room. For a moment I *was* in the front room, then I found myself on the bed again in my bedroom. The experience is difficult to describe. But I know that I was conscious."

Twitchell has often observed that the greatest problem in dealing with this particular aspect of spiritual phenomena is that it has received a lot of drubbing at the hands of its critics. "The semantics of the experience only tend to confuse people," Paulji complained. "Hardly any of those who are able to exteriorize speak the same language. This lack of a suitable vocabulary to communicate the wonder of the experience is the reason why many mystics 'talk' to each other by means of hand language rather than by speech. Language has never been able to describe the wonders that they have seen while traveling in the spiritual worlds."

Why would one want to travel in the soul body?

Spiritual freedom, is Paul Twitchell's answer. "The basic aspect of Eckankar is the liberation from the physical body. Once the individual has learned bilocation—and more importantly, soul travel—he is free to come and go as he wishes in the spirit form. When death occurs he can leave the physical body freely and enter into the spiritual worlds to be with his loved ones who have passed on before him, or he can live where he feels it is best fitted for his spiritual temperament."

The removal of the fear of death has often been commented upon by those who are able to accomplish out-of-the-body experiences. Such an apprehension was reportedly removed from the mother of one of Paulji's *chelas* by the catalyst of bilocation.

"She [the mother] said that she didn't die, she just left her body and stepped into another room where she met my father, her brothers and sister, her mother, father, and Dad's father [all previously deceased]—they were there to help her and to welcome her into the spirit world. She said, 'Now I know there isn't anything to death. One just leaves the body behind and enters into another room.' I told her I was very happy for her, because very few people were given the privilege of experiencing their own

87

ascension before it actually took place. Since then she has been detached from her body, and she says it's the funniest feeling to be elsewhere watching herself sit or do things. She has lost her fear of death, because she has experienced in the astral body what she will eventually experience in the physical world. . ."

And what of the spiritual travelers? Do they actually participate in guiding *chelas* out of the soul body, as Paul Twitchell claims they do?

A Miss P.E.B. of Buffalo, New York, said in December of 1966: "Last night I was concentrating, trying to do what you said. Then I heard a voice asking: 'Do I have your permission to take you out of the body?'

"I said, 'Yes.' Then I must have fallen asleep. Suddenly I felt as if something had hit me on the chest, just under the breastbone, and I heard a loud pop. I nearly lost consciousness again. My heart began to beat very fast. What in the name of God was this?

"I was really afraid to go back to sleep . . . toward the end of my sleep . . . I saw an image and heard a voice say, 'This is Rebazar Tarzs!'

"This really shook me. Was it only my subconscious?"

A very good question, and one which many readers must be asking themselves by now. Is it only a trick of the subconscious which makes one seem to be able to soar through space as a spirit?

World-renowned psychoanalyst C.G. Jung once related an astral projection of his own while he was confined to bed with a heart ailment. "Once it seemed to me that I was high up in space. Far below, I saw the globe of the earth, bathed in a gloriously blue light. I saw the deep blue sea and the continents. . . . It was not a product of imagination. The visions and experiences were utterly real; there was nothing subjective about them; they all had a quality of absolute objectivity."

In tests conducted under laboratory conditions, certain of those who claim to be able to project themselves astrally have been able to accurately describe geographical locations which they had never seen in their physical bodies. Others have given accounts of scenes witnessed and homes visited, which have been corroborated through subsequent investigation.

Certainly, in some cases astral projection must be seen as a product of the imagination, but it appears from the evidence currently being gathered that such a seemingly far-out phenomenon as astral projection may indeed have a physical and objective reality.

Such an objective reality may be illustrated by this letter from a young serviceman who is serving with the armed forces overseas.

". . . I had my first conscious out-of-physical-body experience yesterday morning. I have been studying your discourses for about two months, and at times I have begun to grow discouraged.

"The experience began with . . . *someone* lifting me off the floor . . . I then decided to lighten myself and take control . . . I floated up and away, through a wall and ceiling. The experience was real, but the setting was as in a dream. I don't understand this yet.

"I progressed to another stage where someone massaged my feet, apparently to keep me calm. Suddenly I entered a blackness in which I seemed to move rapidly. Then I heard my mother walking. . . My eyes were closed, yet I heard everything like I used to when I was still at home. I was lying on my bed upstairs. Mother opened the staircase door, and I withdrew . . . I did not want to frighten her as I did not know what my body's constancy was . . .

". . . I returned again to my home bed when she shut the door. She switched on the dining room light and called, '*Essen . . . essen!*' That's German for 'eat'! Apparently my father was asleep on the couch after finishing morning chores on our farm.

"Then I left the house. Even while on my bed at home, I was conscious of someone continuing to massage my feet. The next instant, I was back in my barracks in Japan . . ."

The young soldier overseas may have something in common with a young prisoner behind bars in that both have been removed from their home environment by a force or a situation outside of their control. Bilocation may, therefore, have a similar appeal to individuals who have been separated from their loved ones or from freedom.

A Mr. C.L., who is serving time in the Colorado State Prison, has been passing much of his enforced leisure by studying Paul Twitchell's "Illuminated Way Discourses." C.L. writes that he was relaxing on his bunk after the noon meal when he suddenly found himself in his ". . . light body walking on the guard's catwalk. I could see out over Canon City. Then I began to approach the guard on duty, and it occurred to me what he would think if he could see me up there. The idea struck me as funny, and I started to laugh . . . and zing! Instantly I was back in my body . . . laughing out loud."

In an article which appeared in the September 1965 issue of *Search* magazine, Paulj gave brief instructions on how one might accomplish elementary bilocation.

"One of the simple techniques which I have developed over the years is one I call 'The Easy Way.' Just before going to bed at night sit in an easy chair or on the floor, back erect, and concentrate the attention on the spiritual eye, that place between the eyebrows, while chanting the AUM, or God, inwardly and silently. Hold the attention on a black screen in the inner vision, and keep it free from any pictures if at all possible. If you need a substitute for any mental pictures flashing up unwantedly, place the image of

Christ, or some saint, or a holy man that you know, in place of them.

"After a few minutes of this, suddenly there will come a faint clicking sound in one ear, or the sound of a cork popping, and you will find yourself outside the body looking back at the physical one in the room, and ready for a short journey in the other worlds.

"There is nothing to fear, for no harm can come to you while outside the body, nor to it when left behind. A teacher or guru will be standing by, although you may not know it, to keep watch over your progress. After a while the spirit body will return and slide gently into the body with hardly more than a very light jolt.

"If not successful the first time, try it again, for the technique works. It has worked for others.

"Most of those in the workshop at the California Parapsychology Foundation have learned to do bilocation. So can anyone else who really wishes to learn this ancient art of spiritual phenomenon."

7. Reading the Akashic Records of Past Lives

Sri Paul Twitchell has long been known for his ability to give readings of the "soul records" of past lives which have been impressed on the Great Akasha, or the Divine Consciousness. These soul records consist of past incarnations on the physical, astral, causal, etheric, and soul planes.

"A person who has the ability to do soul travel on his own usually has the talent to read the *Atma*[soul] archives," Twitchell said. "Without casting aspersions on any other type of life readings which are prevalent today, we find that the *Atma* reading is far more revealing for those who desire knowledge of their past lives."

According to Paulji, he learned to read his own soul records while he was projected in his *Atma Sarup* (soul body) with his mentor, Rebazar Tarzs. There, on the fifth plane, the soul plane, the Tibetan pointed out Twitchell's past lives, ". . . which looked like a fan of playing cards spread over the table and which were around my soul like an arc of pictures. These soul embodiments of past lives resembled tiny file cards. Each life had a series of these pictures beginning at birth and passing through all events to death."

When Paulji returned to his physical body, he was able to retain what had been given him of his past lives in the soul records. "Almost anyone who has become proficient at soul travel can read the records of those who request it." Twitchell explained. "He bypasses the aberrations of the readee to reach the higher consciousness and give all that is possible to whom he is reading. However, it must be remembered that since these records must be transferred into the physical language via the physical senses, the readings will have a certain amount of constriction when given, and they should be considered in this light."

"Don't your clients, or readees, express some reluctance to having you peruse their former lives?" I wondered. "If you and certain adepts are able to read these soul records, as you claim to be able to, isn't there a danger of your becoming involved with the reading to the extent that you may inject elements of your own personality into the readings or interfere in some way with the psyche of the readee?"

"For one thing," Paulji answered, "I do not look at the records of another unless I am asked to do so. To look at the records of another without permission is a severe violation of spiritual law!

"The higher one climbs on the spiritual ladder, the more will he grant others their own freedom and give less interference to another's state of consciousness.

"As we mount the scale upward the more ethical we become in our conduct. We will not make any attempt to discuss or assist in anyone's problem unless asked to do so, for according to spiritual law, the individual consciousness of a person is his home. A spiritual traveler cannot enter unless invited."

"But isn't it a bit of a temptation not to become a bit 'preachy' perhaps, if you have read the past lives of someone who was, or is, a real louse?" I asked. "And if you see a man's problems all laid out in such a manner, isn't it a bit difficult not to become involved?"

"I'm certain that it might have been so at one time," Paulji admitted, "but the reader of the soul records always practices *Vairag* [emotional and mental detachment] for those whom he is

93

investigating these records. Under no circumstances can he become involved in the problems of others unless he is asked to assist."

"Paulji," I said, "since I wrote that chapter on your reading of the soul records for my *The Enigma of Reincarnation*, the publisher, you, and I have all been deluged with mail."

"Yes," Twitchell smiled. "One Monday my secretary found that over a thousand letters had piled up over the weekend."

"In that chapter, as you will recall," I went on, "we mentioned the laws of *Karma*. Many of the letters which I received from readers asked for a further explanation of what is meant by this concept of the laws of retribution. Could you, for the readers of this book, deal with *Karma* at some length?"

"Certainly," Paulji agreed. "Actually, *Karma* is a very simple aspect of divine nature. It is hardly anything more than the law of cause and effect. Somewhere, sometime, we start an action that must later appear as effect in our life—whether it is in this life or in some future incarnation. This is the law, and as long as we live in the lower worlds, it must be obeyed.

"*Karma* goes under many names—the law of retribution, the law of compensation, Yang and Yin, and many others. It is the practice of payment for the fixed law of nature.

"With reincarnation, *Karma* is the twin doctrine of life and the very result of all concerned with this life on the physical plane, the astral and causal planes, and all planes in the lower worlds. Both doctrines are concerned with the life of the individual up to the soul plane, the fifth region of God."

"Why reincarnation?" I interrupted. "Why do you maintain that the soul continues a cycle of rebirth?"

"Each soul must serve in the lower worlds in order to gain spiritual purification," Paulji said. "God sent us here from out of the heavenly kingdom as untried souls to gain this purification. We are like children who must attend school to get simulated experiences to prepare us for a place in our society. The lower worlds serve as a kind of school to spiritually educate our souls. Eventually, after many incarnations, soul is purified by its experiences and rids itself of the lower universe *Karma* via reincarnations on the Wheel of the Eighty-four."

"The Wheel of the Eighty-four," I echoed. "Are you now referring to the zodiac?"

"Right you are," Twitchell smiled."The *Awagawan*, where we must spend so many incarnations in each zodiacal sign in order to overcome the influences of the cycles of birth and death. The eighty-four on the wheel means the number of times we will have births and deaths in the lower worlds. Some souls will have to go through each zodiac sign as many as seven times in order to conquer the influences outside of itself."

"When you say 'some' you must be implying that the process can be accelerated," I said.

"This is true," Paulji noted. "One does not have to spend this eternity in a round of births and deaths if he learns to follow a path of total awareness of God which will lead him through *Karma.* One such path would, of course, be that of Eckankar."

"We've digressed a bit," I said, "and it has been my fault. May we return to a discussion of *Karma* itself?"

Paulji nodded. "I should mention that there are four types of *Karma.* First, there is the *Adi Karma*, which is the primal *Karma.* It consists of the action of the creative force, the *Bani*, whose function it is to take the soul from its original home to the material plane so it can begin to accumulate experience on its own initiative.

"Second is that called the *Prarabdh Karma*, which means fate *Karma. Prarabdh* is that which has been earned in one or more previous lives and which one's present life is based upon.

"Third is *Sinchit Karma*, reserve *Karma*, which might be compared to a savings account which can be drawn upon at the will of the Lords of *Karma*. This means that the individual may be assigned to live out his *Karma* in the place and the time that the Lords of the *Karma* may determine. The person so affected has nothing to say about it.

"The fourth kind of *Karma* is that which is called *Kryiman Karma*, the daily *Karma* we make and work out. It is *Kryiman Karma* which we are making each moment from day to day in this life. We can rid ourselves of it by suffering and reaping such rewards as might accrue from chaste and moderate living.

"All *Karma* may be broken by passing into the higher worlds via soul travel; once soul enters into these higher worlds, it becomes a free agent and is permitted to roam the worlds as it pleases, so long as such journeying is in the best interest of all concerned.

"All spiritual travelers may break the *Karma* of any *chelas*—and for anyone as far as that goes—but it is always best to leave *Karma* alone in people unless there is a true necessity for breaking it. Each person must go through a lot of his own *Karma* for the purpose of learning and experiencing life.

"No truly wise master will take on the *Karma* of another person, for by so doing, he would only add the *chela's Karma* to his own and, consequently, would have to pay for it himself. All *Karma* must be paid for by each individual soul; therefore, no spiritual traveler is actually interested in the *Karma* of anyone else, except to see that his *chelas* may be guided in the right direction."

Again, Sri Paul Twitchell opened his files to me. I read hundreds of letters from those who had requested readings of their Akashic records and who had responded with such comments as:

"*After receiving the reading and studying it very*

thoroughly, I have noted a substantial improvement in my outlook and my ability to maintain a steadier level of emotional stability, so it has been of distinct benefit as well as of interest."

"I found the entire reading both intriguing and enlightening."

"The reading has changed my outlook on life and on myself. I think I now understand what is meant by recognizing that God is here and now and not somewhere far off to be sought for."

"Last February you did my Akashic reading and it was wonderful! Previously I had been meeting with deep frustration all through my life, but now this frustration doesn't seem to bother me so much, and I don't get depressed like I used to."

Paul Twitchell maintains that each of us has lived not just one previous life, but that we have experienced many prior incarnations. Whether or not one chooses to believe such an allegation is, of course, up to the individual. Paulji would be the first to point out that all decisions of spiritual nature must be made on a personal and individual basis. In matters of the spirit, one must balance the scales with his own conscience and the stuff of his own soul.

Whether one is skeptical toward such concepts as the Akashic records or whether he is a true believer in their existence, nearly everyone must admit to some curiosity regarding a reading of the Akasha. Sri Paul Twitchell has herewith permitted me to publish excerpts from three Akashic readings to demonstrate to the readers of this book exactly what is meant by an examination of one's past lives via projection of the soul body. The cases which are quoted are those of active Twitchell *chelas*. For obvious reasons, all references to real names and actual places have been omitted.

"It is my pleasure to have this opportunity to do

your Akashic reading via soul projection.

"I wish to point out here that you are surrounded by a light rose and silvery light which emerges into the space around you. It is sometimes called the magnetic field; some call it the aura, but it is really the colors emitted from soul. It also means that you are living on two planes, in the physical and spiritual consciousness. The old expression, 'My heart is in heaven but my feet are on earth' can be applied to you. This is not unusual for anyone, who like yourself, is interested in the study of the spiritual works. This is often called the dual consciousness.

"Many who have progressed to the higher planes seldom recognize this within themselves while the physical senses are in charge of the individual. Again I point out that this is not an unusual state for we look too much to situations in the outer world and not to the inner world.

"At the start of this reading I wish to say that you will be given some of the major incarnations in which your many lives were spent on earth. To get them all down would take days and reams of paper, so I will discuss those lives which, in my opinion, are important to you here and now, as the result of your *Karma;* and if you wish to take up any particulars and have any questions I will gladly discuss them with you.

"The reason we are here on earth instead of heaven is simply that we are sent here from the God-realm as untried souls into this physical universe to gain experiences, as children must attend school to get an education. Eventually, after many incarnations, soul is purified by its experiences, and it returns to heaven where it is ready to serve God and become a co-worker with the Deity.

"Each time we take up a new body here on earth, soul retains the memory patterns of its lives in past bodies. But the new brain does not have any memory of these past lives. Once this happens our sojourn here is practically over, and we are aware of who we are and what our goal is, and we start working to get back into heaven again.

"You came to earth with the idea that something could be done to help the human race. But it was a failure, something to be expected when one is working with the human consciousness. You were reborn in the ancient country of Hekra, which in our modern times is known as Spain. It was in the southwestern corner near the Pyrenees mountains. You were a young priestess of the Fire Cult at the time, and served in the temple, where the chief priest was a ruthless, dictatorial kind of person. The elder prince, son of the ruler, wanted you as a bride, but the priest had no intentions of giving you up, for your father was a wealthy man and could give much money to the religious order to which you and the chief priest belonged. So you became a pawn of a game that was fought between the two factions. Finally the prince saw he wasn't going to get you away from the priest legally, for his father wouldn't help, so he decided to kidnap you. It turned into a tragedy. During a raid on the temple, he was killed and you got the blame. The king believed it was your fault so he had you killed. It turned out that after your death he learned the truth.

"This was your first incarnation on earth, and for the first time, you encountered the lower consciousness. That state of mind which deals with all the low negative forces, like intrigue, death, unhappiness, and force. The Lords of *Karma* placed you in this position to start your life *Karma*, of which some aspects are showing up in this present life. Some of the people in this first incarnation are members of your family—near relatives and friends who are working out their *Karma* with you also. This sort of human relationship must go on until it has been dissolved either by an ECK master or it has done so of itself, by gradually giving up its hold on you because of a limited area of time that *Karma* can hold to soul. I would say that you will be rid of this *Karma* within this lifetime, perhaps in five years or so.

"Your next incarnation of any importance which is showing up in this lifetime was during the time of Christ. You were a good friend of young Mark, who later became known as St. Mark. You were a witness to the incident in which Christ was arrested and Mark lost his robe as he fled. You also ran with him to escape the soldiers and arrest. You saw the trial and crucifixion. It never dawned upon you at the time what this was all about, but later, when Mark went to Egypt, you became interested and would have followed, except for an illness resulting from a disease that swept the countryside in an epidemic.

"This illness was a part of your *Karma*, showing up from former lives in which the *Karmic* pattern was resulting from deep nervous troubles. This was that part of the *Karma* which led to a defeatist attitude and ill-health in this life. It has led to a position of having an impasse, a blind alley today. Because you were so discouraged over the ending of this life in such a bitter way, it has become a pattern that has followed you down through other lives into this life. You did not find the teachings at this time, because of a lack of awareness of what Christ was trying to tell the people. This has caused you to wander about for many lives until you have come into this one. You will find that many of these *Karmic* patterns of the past will now start dissolving, and your future will be faced with greater happiness and with greater confidence. It will start being a pleasure to live again.

"The next important life that you lived was during the time of the Second Crusade in France, when all the world was afire to win over the Holy Lands from the Turks and Eastern races. It was another time when you were in the form of a young man who was too sensitive for the age and who was bitterly treated by life, because of your *Karmic* debt. This time you became the member of the armed forces of the crusades, as a young priest who was to receive the confessions of the troops before each battle. You were also a sort of a rude medical man, who bound up the wounds and prayed over the dying and dead. It was a rough, harsh life, and nothing in it gave you satisfaction unless it was the belief that you were in God's work. You were captured by the Moslems in the Holy Land and sold into slavery. This life led to your death, for you couldn't stand the hard, physical strain, and the lack of good food.

"This was one of the worst incarnations that you have had, and it has affected your present life through easily fatiguing depressions, and feeling of a lack of freedom around some people."

"You were born on this Earth planet during the era of the Chou dynasty in China. This was a feudalist society in which you were one of the Wu priests. The Wu clergy, or priests, were those known for their ability to aid in healing and doing magic spells. It was a sad life for you, because as a man interested in justice for all people, you had to be very careful how your behavior was conducted and what you said. This was too bad, for you really wanted to help the underprivileged and poor. It was a rough life under the circumstances, but you were very discreet. Yet there were times when you spoke out of order, only to have the secret agents of the king mark up points against you. Finally it all came to a head when, annoyed beyond endurance, you asked for an audience with the king, only to appear before him to denounce his policy in taxing the poor heavier than the rich. This was your downfall. The king ordered your arrest, and after a trial which was mockery, had you beheaded.

"This was an era in which the Lords of *Karma* assigned your *Karma* for this earthly world. You fell victim to treachery and unhappiness in the human consciousness. But then it is the way of the lower worlds to inflict punishment upon anyone or anything that does not agree with its policy of cruelty and hardships. This trait of helping others, or feeling sympathetic for them, has followed you down through the years over the many lives spent here.

"You have come down through a large number of incarnations to a life just previous to this one. This was during the time of the Civil War in which you served as a nurse under Clara Barton, who formed the first Red Cross. Being a refined young woman, the horror and unsanitary conditions of the hospitals were sickening. Here you found a young officer in the Union army, nursed him to health, married, and moved west to ranch. He was killed in an Indian raid in West Texas, shortly after moving into this vicinity. You were compelled to manage the ranch and raise your three sons. It was a life of hardship, but a noble one for your dedication and loyalty to those children. Two of them died at an early age, but the other grew into adulthood and passed away about age thirty from a gun wound.

"The young officer was your husband in this life. The health problems he has comes out of this era. During the Italian era he was another man who was in love with you and was very sad when you went into a convent. He has been with you in each of the incarnations as father, friend, and kin. Of course he has been with you in many others that are not discussed here. Only a few of your incarnations have been given, for the ones named are concerned with your health problems and emotional states. But as I pointed out before, many of these are leaving you. You will be entering into a new life soon, both of you. That is a higher spiritual life. In doing so many

102

of these problems and *Karmic* debts will be wiped out. This should start working out so you can see some results within the next six months."

"Now the next life in which you had an important incarnation for the accumulation of your *Karmic* debt was during the time of Darius the Great, king of Persia. You lived in Babylon after its capture by the Persians, as a young temple priestess in the temple of Marduk, the greatest of gods. Taken captive you were sent back to the palace of Darius to be a slave, woman and work in the kitchen. This was perhaps the harshest time in your whole lives. It was one in which you suffered terribly from humiliations and brutality. You had to keep yourself free as much as possible under the conditions that availed. But you were a slave, and being a slave, you were subjected to every embarrassment capable in a human being. You finally died from exhaustion and semistarvation. Although you worked around the kitchen, too often the overseer would not let you eat as punishment for some minor infraction of his rules.

"The *Karmic* condition gathered in this particular lifetime was one which you had little to do with, but you were caught in the web of another soul, one who was working out much of his own. This particular soul was the overseer in the kitchen, who caused your death, and he has been around you for the last two incarnations of your life—the present one and the one just before it. It is one of your near kin. This *Karma* is being worked out now and will not bother you again in any future life, if you have to have one.

"The next important incarnation was during the time of the golden age in Florence, Italy, when artists were being made great. You were an apprentice artist but never got anywhere with the work, for when the French captured the city in 1494 you fled with several artists, including Michelangelo.

"We are now running into the same trait, that which has brought about anger resulting from a feeling of inadequacy. You had real artistic talent, but being made an errand boy for a genius certainly wasn't conducive to your welfare and talent. This created frustration and anger, because you didn't seem to be getting anywhere. It created tension, ill health, and unhappiness, and certainly a lack of finances. This meant that you were always in bad health over the upsets which ruined your digestion, and the bad food which made it worse. As a result, if you hadn't gone out the way you did, you would have taken on an emotional disease and passed away at an early age.

"Next we find you in a very important incarnation, during the time of the bloody years of the French terror following the revolution. You were a young schoolteacher who had taught the children of the nobility until the overthrow of the government. The king was executed and all royalty put to death or forced to flee the country. You went in hiding and were comparatively safe, but the Jacobins wanted you because they believed that you knew where the famous necklace of Marie Antoinette was hidden. It had disappeared when she was arrested, and it could not be found. You were finally caught and tortured, but not knowing where the necklace could be found, you had no information to give the captors. You died under torture and your body was flung in a shallow grave.

"This was a frustrating and unhappy era in which you saw violence and bloodshed which led to nothing but more unhappiness. It was a time that you had to live through in order to be cleansed of some of the past *Karma*, but, on the other hand, you gathered new fears of bloodshed and violence. It was a time of never being able to accomplish anything, for you had a love of children and were on the verge of marriage when the revolution broke out and left you hunted and childless, full of terror of men and their awful deeds.

"Please do not feel that all your *Karma* was filled with bloodshed and violence, for there were many lifetimes when you had good periods; but you are being shown what the life *Karma* on the negative side has pulled up for you and must be rid of before you go into the other worlds for good. You must go through all of these fears, frustrations, and unhappiness in order to be polarized into the positive side."

8.   Healing in the Soul Body

Paul Twitchell receives as many as four thousand letters a week from unhappy people in practically every country in the world, including many from such Iron Curtain countries as Austria, East Germany, Poland, Czechoslovakia, and Hungary. Perhaps the great majority of these letters request Paulji's spiritual help in combating a disease or a serious illness.

As I was in the process of preparing this book, I was allowed to examine the extensive files of Sri Paul Twitchell. I cannot personally testify that the spiritual adept actually projects himself in some manner to those who request his ministrations, but when one reads the stacks of testimonials it soon becomes apparent that thousands of people *are* willing to give Paulji credit for their healings.

That which is popularly called "faith healing" is a strange and often wonderful phenomenon, and many learned men have long debated first, whether such a thing does indeed exist, and second, whether it is the healer who heals or if it is the act of belief on the part of the ill which performs the miracle. In other words, I have no way of knowing whether Paulji travels all over the world in his soul body to accomplish these alleged cures or if it is the faith which his supplicants have in his powers that brings about their own cures.

All I can personally testify to is that I have read a great many letters in which the writers give unsolicited and unequivocal praise to Sri Paul

Twitchell and deem him fully responsible for their present state of well-being.

"I appreciate the help I received in regard to my present operation," reads a letter from a Mrs. G.V. of Missouri. "I am getting along so well that my doctor is aghast at the quick healing and my ability to get around. . ."

A Miss T.C. of Brooklyn hails Paulji as her "Beloved Guardian Angel" and details how ECK has cured her of becoming an alcoholic. "I couldn't pass up an offer of a drink ever," she writes. "I couldn't pass a bar without sampling not one or two, but seven or eight!" Then, after the spirit of ECK flowed into her, she had ". . . absolutely no desire for one drink, which is to me a miracle! All of my troubles and problems have fallen away, just as you said they would, dearest guru. I used to have a death wish, now you make my life worth living!"

Did Paulji's *Atma Sarup* really travel to West Germany to prompt this response from a skeptic, or is it only some dynamic power of auto-suggestion? "I was very skeptical, but I am glad to say that a good beginning has been achieved and I am longing for my complete recovery. Therefore I beg you to continue your efforts in healing my appalling illness of muscular dystrophy. At the same time, I thank you very much for all the goodness I'll receive from the spiritual gift of healing."

"None can be refused," Paulji said, "for my responsibility as a channel for the Spirit of God is to give to anyone who asks. I, of myself, do not heal, but it is Spirit flowing through me, using me as a channel. Spirit makes Its own choice of whom It will heal. I can make no guarantees of success. The innate wisdom of Spirit knows better than anyone in the human state of consciousness what is best for each individual."

A cross section of the people who write to Sri Paul

Twitchell with problems to be solved would include clergymen, nuns, sisters, and lay members of many different orders. Nearly every occupation and profession seemed to be represented in the letters which I examined, everything from postal employees and poets, to physicists and pharmacists.

Many of those who write to Paulji request the solution of one specific problem which they believe hinders them from a more abundant life, but, the guru pointed out, Spirit in Its greater wisdom knows better and takes care of what must really be done.

"Recently a man wrote to me requesting spiritual assistance for financial help," Twitchell said. "He claimed that a specific job was needed to help his economic situation. A few months later, I received a letter from him in which he complained that nothing had been done for him. He neglected to mention that his health had certainly been improved!

"I had to explain to him that Spirit, in all Its wisdom, knew that he needed good health first, for without this necessary factor, it would have been impossible to even think of going after that new job. A later letter from this gentleman told me that he had accepted a position with an excellent business firm. He expected to be successful, since he was now in such a vigorous state of health. Spirit, of course, had foreseen this chain of events and knew that good health must come before a better job."

Among the thousands of letters that reach Sri Paul Twitchell's desk each week, the guru has noted three basic problems: the fear of death, the fear of poverty, and the fear of poor health.

The key to these three human life problems, Twitchell feels, is simply this: "That all who put their faith and trust in human nature are constantly disappointed and find little happiness.

"It seems strange that throughout the ages every known religion, all mystics, spiritual teachers, and

108

holy men of all countries, have emphasized the basic cardinal principle to have faith in God, but few have adhered to it." Paulji frowned.

"Once I approached Sri Sudar Singh, my first ECK master in his *ashram* at Allahabad, India, with a number of questions about the spiritual affairs of man, only to hear him say: 'You have no need of questions. Trust God!'"

Trust in God is the only security that we have in life, Twitchell believes. "Trust in God" is the answer to all three basic problems that confront the human race today.

"The majority of the human race quiver and shake at the thought of death," Paulji observed. "This is shown in a letter received from a woman who has reached middle age, and now faces the older years."

"Dear Blessed Paul Twitchell:

"Please forgive me for writing but it is necessary that I find peace of mind. My problem is that I am within two years of reaching that state called old age, and dread it, for it means that I am close to death and fearful of what lies beyond it. "Is there some way that I can have relief from this awful fear? It haunts me day and night, and certainly I am not prepared to meet the angel of death."

Paulji readily saw that this woman certainly had a problem. Like many persons she either had not had a true religious foundation, or she had forgotten and neglected the basic principles which she had been taught during her youth.

Twitchell's reply to her went like this:

"My Dear One:

"What you have said in your letter is often true

109

of people who have reached your age. Mainly, they feel they have no future, and when one loses the dreams and visions of his former years, all is gone and depression replaces hope.

"Please let me assure you here that your future is brighter and more secure than you can believe possible. When we step across the border that separates the invisible from the visible, it is then we have conquered death in the truest sense.

"However, here I do suggest that you get busy with some project, mainly with children if at all possible. Find someone's children; orphans, grandchildren, or others to help with. It is so much fun to watch growing things, especially the human young. You will find something to do with your hands and mind within a reasonable time. I predict this for you."

A few weeks later a reply from the woman said that a foundling home had accepted her as a voluntary worker and that she was extremely happy among these tiny tots who needed the loving care that she had to give.

An example of the second type of problem is shown in the following letter on a fear of poverty.

"Dear Friend:

"I am a man of forty-five, responsible for a family and respected in my community. But I have been dismissed from the firm which employed me for the last fifteen years as a bookkeeper because the employer believed a younger man could do the work faster and cheaper.

"I am writing you because there is no place to turn. Nobody wants a man of my age. Can you give me spiritual help?"

Paul's reply to him was this:

"Dear Beloved Friend:

"In the time of a crisis man always turns to God. Now you have asked for spiritual help through me, acting as a channel for Divine Spirit.

"It is quite absurd to tell you not to have anxieties since there are others whom you are responsible for. But please be assured that God does not forget once you turn to Him.

"I feel that while you are looking for employment you should take up accounting work at some night school. This will give you an added advantage when talking to employers and will help you hold a job for years where a bookkeeper's experience won't. However, I do want you to know that the rightful job is awaiting you, and will soon be found."

Another letter arrived several days later saying that he had followed Twitchell's suggestion of enrolling in a night course in accounting. But his main news was that his old firm had requested that he return to take over the department of accounting. The head accountant had retired and they had no one as experienced, nor as qualified as himself to manage this department. In addition, he got a fine raise in salary and a management job when the firm heads learned that he had begun study in accounting.

The next universal problem of man is the fear of poor health, which is portrayed in the following letter:

"Dear Blessed One:

"I desire spiritual help from you about my health problem. Being a widow, I must work for a living, and for the last few months my health has gone down badly due to worry over bills, job, and the general state of affairs that our country is in. Please give me some sort of help."

The reply was:

"Dear Madam:

"I do appreciate the state of affairs that you have described in your letter. My suggestion here is that you give up all these problems to God, and let Him dissolve them. Further, I suggest that you have the proper physical examination to see that no damage has been done for the future, by worry and general unhappiness. Health is the first thing that we must think about in our search for peace of mind and earning ability. Unless we have it, many unnecessary sufferings come to us. But once you give up and put your trust in God the peace of mind returns and your state of affairs will be much better."

Her reply some time later said that she had decided it was better to give up to God and to trust in Him. A physical examination relieved her mind of any further health problem. She was now happier and felt as if a real achievement had been made in her life, because God had taken over and was directing it.

Once when visiting Sri Rebazar Tarzs, the great Tibetan master of Eckankar, in his little hut in the western Himalayan mountains, Twitchell asked how one should go about finding God in his life.

The holy man smiled broadly and replied, "Sit still and do something!"

This was an odd answer, but he would not elaborate, so Paulji was left to work out his own interpretation of what was being said there in the cold, clear heights of the world's highest mountains.

Later Paulji learned that Rebazar Tarzs was speaking of the endless problems that most of man face daily: "That is, the tendency toward inertia, of the sluggishness and inability to do something, in either the spiritual or physical spheres of our lives.

"The lack of energy to accomplish what we set out to do is a restriction to getting the most out of living. We all complain of the senseless nature of our lives, which seems at variance with our whole purpose in living, but we never do anything about it. Defeats create losses and we are shot downward into the lower states of apathy, unhappiness, and frustration. We lose whatever drive is needed to succeed at winning what is the simplest necessity in life.

"Then I began to understand what Rebazar Tarzs was speaking of that fine spring morning in his little mud hut in the high peaks of central Asia. Many spiritual masters will act in the same manner, in never replying directly to our questions. They want us to learn how to get the answers ourselves.

"I learned that such frustrations and losses may have two, and sometimes three reactions on the individual. First, they create a feeling of helplessness and one becomes a victim of his own states of consciousness and outer circumstances.

"Secondly, they may reverse the pattern of helplessness and stir up an immense psychic power within one which creates aggressiveness toward individuals and masses of people. This occurs frequently in marriages where one mate has reached a point of helplessness in trying to act as an equal in the marital state, but his failures have turned into aggressiveness toward his marriage partner. Many of our historical leaders, Napoleon, Kublai Khan, Hitler, Alexander the Great, Cortez, and hundreds of others, are examples of those who became victims of the aggressive reactions of restricted lives during their earlier years. The bloody pages of history are proof of this.

"Thirdly, if such frustrations stir the higher spiritual forces in one's life, he may become an inspired leader to lift others into the higher levels of spiritual understanding. He becomes an inspiration to many in far corners of the world who will never see nor know him personally. These forces act as a catalytic agent to jerk him out of the doldrums into a position of leadership that takes individuals and masses upward into inspired lives.

"Many of those who write are made cripples by the forces of the negative power, and are driven into deep inertia which keeps them from becoming persons useful to one another."

One such letter came to Sri Paul Twitchell's attention recently.

"My Dear Master:

"It grieves me to have to write and ask for help. But I am helpless from a lack of energy, many feelings of guilt, and the knack of doing nothing. I feel all right, but just do not want to do anything for myself and family. My children avoid me and my husband says that I am like a bump on a log. My appearance has gone to pot. I am a good Christian but don't even like to pray any more."

My reply to this woman was:

"Dear Madam:

"You are trapped in the negative power, which loves to use people in this manner. Your guilt problems are arising because you are used to doing for your family, in numerous domestic ways, but now since this terrible inertia has set

114

in you have met with nothing but defeat and losses. Even your children who were used to your love and happiness in preparing for them have lost respect. Your husband no longer cares, since you have let yourself run down.

"I suggest that you cease the worrying about what has happened to you, and have physical action. Go shopping, buy a new dress and hat. Pretty up and go to church on Sunday, but take the family with you. Cook a good dinner tonight. Show them that mother is alive, well, and happy.

"Next I suggest that twice a day you sit very still in a quiet room and recite to yourself, very slowly, the Lord's Prayer or the Twenty-Third Psalm. Within a few days you will see the change in yourself; a vigorous, loving mother of whom your family will be proud."

Later her reply told Paulji that his suggestions had been followed and that she was now freed of the guilt patterns created by that terrible feeling of no-action. This woman had learned that once the spiritual forces were released within, her whole life would be changed for the better.

"Although we dislike to admit it," Paulji said, "Black magic is on the rampage throughout the world today. It is even being practiced by many who are innocent of having the least notion that they practice such dark magic on others. I am more convinced of this every day by observing the developments of the world today and by the contents of the thousands of letters that flow across my desk weekly. Those who dabble in black magic in order to get a fulfillment of their wishes in the materialist sense are putting themselves into a mire from which it is hard to be extracted. Black magic has a way of holding to its practitioners.

"Black magic is use of mind power to gain an objective in the physical universe. It is usually done by force and mental strength against another's will or to move objects into one's own orbit for self-comfort and indulgence.

"White magic is use of spiritual power to gain an objective in the spiritual universes. It is usually done by giving up one's own will to God's desire for him, and by following this desire regardless of where the path may lie and whatever the hardships may be.

"Those who practice black magic are self-indulgent followers of the negative power. Whether they understand it or not, there will come a reckoning sooner or later, because the psychic, that which we often call the negative power, is not a stable force, like the positive, or the spiritual power. The practitioner will go down the scale of life to that which is not to his liking, in both health and economics. Then he will suffer the same in proportion to those whom he has brought under his own domination and control.

"I often have letters from people who claim that they are victims of black magic, or who want me to use the power of divine spirit to put another under their control. Such requests usually come from those who are completely ignorant of the mechanics of spirit."

One such letter went like this:

"Dear Master:

"Please grant my prayer that the woman I was to marry return to me. We were to be married but had several harsh quarrels and broke up. Now she won't even see me when I go to her house, or answer the telephone. Please make her love me, for if she doesn't return my love, I know that I shall die."

This was a clear-cut case of someone wanting to use black magic to gain love against the will of the other person. Paulji's reply was very simple and to the point.

"My Dear Friend:

"I wish to inform you that it would be against the Will of God for me to use any power that He so grants me, to change another person to suit the desires of anyone.

"Since God has given us all free will I suggest that you be patient, and give the young lady a chance to make up her mind. Pushing her to decide will not help matters, not even praying that she will, helps. If she decides to do so, let her do it willingly on her own, otherwise if you do get her, what do you have—an unwilling person, who will give you trouble the balance of your marriage.

"It is against the spiritual law to force anyone to do anything whether it is mentally, physically, or spiritually. If I am a party to your plan, then I am as guilty with the spiritual law as you are. Give freedom to all and you will be free."

Sri Paul Twitchell receives many such letters. Some ask for direct domination over others in thought and body; others ask for sexual control over mates and women; a few ask for the power to get money whenever they can, and still others request revenge upon so-called enemies.

Of course Paulji has no objections to persons wanting health and the comforts of life, but he must draw a line against those who want domination and control over others and revenge on whom ever has hurt them or done them an injury.

"This is trying to make use of the spiritual power for a lower deed and will surely make trouble for whoever uses it in this manner," Twitchell remarked. "A traveler on the path to God is certainly not a magician, but one who has heart and mind established on reaching the highest realm of the Supreme Deity."

Paulji says that Rebazar Tarzs was once approached by a man who wanted to have great powers to destroy his enemies. "For what reason?" asked the great ECK master.

"So that I can be free of them," came the reply.

Rebazar Tarzs said, "My dear friend, if you destroy your enemies with such powers, it is quite certain that you would destroy yourself. So I say unto you love them, and they in turn will love you."

The man studied this for a while. "But then they wouldn't be my enemies."

The ECK spiritual master said nothing, but smiled broadly.

Melarepa, the eleventh century Tibetan saint, and member of the ancient order of ECK masters, went through a period of practicing black magic. He was hired by many to destroy their enemies, but he soon learned the consequences of practicing black magic while traveling the spiritual path. None can do it without suffering terrible repercussions in his personal life.

One woman wrote from a foreign country recently saying that she was the victim of another practicing black magic on herself. Sri Paul Twitchell wrote back saying, "Whatever you believe of whoever is doing this, do not think of them as being a practitioner of black magic. Believe instead that this person is incapable of doing harm to anyone.

"No harm can come to you especially if you will put your faith in the fact that I have thrown an armor of protection around you. Not an ounce of harm can come to you now since you are wearing this spiritual shield. I will be with you and protect you at all times.

"Have no thought about the intentions of whoever

118

you think is doing this to you, for within ten days it will all be over and you will be freed of any influence that others might send you. Nothing can touch you."

Her reply to Paulji was that within exactly six days the person who was sending her malignant thoughts stopped, and since then nothing had occurred.

Again, it would seem, the distance of many miles is as nothing to the spiritual power which is alleged to flow through Sri Paul Twitchell.

Phyllis Moore of Denver, Colorado, told me, in regard to a query concerning Paulji's healing talents, "You may say that I was healed of a condition that doctors are not able to cure—adhesions. When doctors try to cure them, they open the abdomen again, and in releasing them, they make other adhesions, just from the surgery. In a few weeks after I had appealed to Paul Twitchell, I was fully out of pain and feeling wonderful. I have not had a single abdominal pain since that time—and it was so bad before that I took several aspirins every day."

Rev. W.R. Harrison of Newfield, New Jersey, wrote to tell me of his healing experience via Paul Twitchell and Eckankar, then added: "If I had a choice between a million dollars and the pathway of ECK, I would choose ECK. Some day the million dollars would be no good to me or could vanish overnight, but what I receive and have learned from following the pathway of ECK, I shall have forever. No power in the heavens would want to take it away from me, and no powers on earth or hell would be able to take it away from me. ECK leads one from the delusions of earthly existence to an understanding of the true, the real, the eternal."

9. A Journey to the "Far Country"

In this chapter we once again approach the mystery of *The Far Country* which we dealt with in Chapter One. Even though Mr. W.R. of New York claimed to have held the materialized volume in his hands and even to have browsed through its text in March of 1966, *The Far Country* remains in manuscript form, and the selections which I shall quote in this chapter will mark the remarkable book's first physical exposure to the printed page.

The manuscript itself is about 90,000 words in length and contains twelve chapters, which deal with such topics as "A Searchlight on Religions," "The Disinterested Works," "The Immortal *Tuza*," "The Rest Points of Eternity," "The Non-Existence of Space," and "The *Sugmad* of Being."

The "Far Country" is a magnificent series of spiritual universes where the *tuza* (soul) goes following the disposal of its earthly body in that phenomenon called death. It is also the land where so many masters and adepts travel in their *Nuri Sarups* (light bodies) from this earth plane.

"Rudyard Kipling wrote a story about a boy who had a glimpse of this Far Country," Twitchell pointed out. "Occasionally the lad would view this vision as he progressed into manhood. He yearned to enter that Far Country, but he had no way except through death. Then, when the visionary is dying from a wound received in battle during World War I, he once again sees the images of the Far Country and he knows that at last he is ready to enter. The short story is entitled 'The Far Country,' and it is one of Kipling's best."

Paulji told me that those who had had a glimpse of the Far Country are always unhappy with their existence on this earth planet, unless they have learned the art of soul travel. Some misguided individuals have even committed suicide in the hope of reaching the Far Country, but such an action, of course, only defeats their purpose.

"It was while traveling with Sudar Singh in the *Nuri Sarup* that I met Rebazar Tarzs," Paulji reminded me, "and it was in the company of Rebazar Tarzs that I returned to study the Far Country. Later, with Gail and her spiritual guide, Dr. John Leland, I came to know Rebazar Tarzs better, and I began to leave my physical body at night to meet with him at his mud and brick hut in the Himalayas. It was a series of twelve important dialogues with Rebazar Tarzs which produced my manuscript *The Far Country*."*

Here, then, are selected passages from that most enigmatic and provocative manuscript.

"No saviour who came to this world intended to propagate a faith. Instead he wanted to relay a certain few truths learned in the Far Country, and pass them along to those who would listen.

"The ancient teachers followed this method. They scarcely wrote anything, for none of the followers had the ability to read. They passed the word by mouth. Once they initiated a person onto the holy path, which they were following, then they would turn to another.

"None had a clinging social teaching as you find today in many of the organized churches. Therefore you find that religion is simply a social institution. This is especially true of the Western religions, and

*Published in 1970.

also a great many of those in the Oriental countries.

"Name one religion which is in existence today, and I will show you that it is a product of social conscience instead of the truth of the *Sugmad* [God]. Therefore, all laws which are called the 'Law of God' are hardly more than the evolution of social conscience from the Law of Manu, Code of Hammurabi, Law of Moses, and the Canons of the Christian Church.

"What do they represent? Hardly more than the rules and regulations of the priestcraft by which they might control their followers and maintain a political and economic hold over the multitudes. Didn't Jesus know this when he was challenged by the Pharisees and Torahists?"

"God appears to all men in the same fashion, regardless of their faith and religion. Those who seek the unknown quality have experiences which are far out of this world. Experiences are worthless; you can have them for a rupee a dozen, or in the thousands if necessary, but what is the use of such a thing?"

"The true spiritual traveler, regardless of what anybody says in any of the planes here or in the Far Country, doesn't seek mystic experiences to better himself, nor is he interested in people or working for the *tuza*.

"He backs away instantly from any authority whatsoever. He calls upon no one, not even the *Sugmad*, for aid, for he knows that it depends upon himself to solve the issues which he must face in the Far Country."

"Reaching the world of the *Sugmad* gives a freedom which is the fulfillment of independence from any restraint whatsoever. This is a condition which encourages and allows for active exercise of the will. No outside interference can possibly change the course of the will, for freedom comes through the *Sugmad* once it has determined its goal.

"The world of *Sugmad* is beyond explanation. None can tell you of its beauty and wonders. This is a world of pure spirit, and the *tuza* that gains a place here becomes pure spirit only.

"It, the *Sugmad*, is the sovereign lord with whom the saints have to collaborate in carrying out their sacred missions of giving the right instructions to *tuzas* who wish to enter this world."

"Billions of years ago there was a mighty deity called the *Sugmad*, known to all the great races of the world. This deity was so powerful that he forbade the worship of Himself as a God. He lived in that world, beyond the reaches of all mankind, but He appeared often upon the physical plane for proof that He was a living being.

"During His sojourn upon this plane, He explained carefully to the leaders of the races that He existed because they allowed Him to exist. Otherwise He had no form, no shape, nor any facilities which could be used in transmitting His ideas to men, provided they didn't furnish Him with them.

"In other words He could manifest to men only if they would make use of their creative energies, for it was only through this faculty that he came to this planet. If enough would believe and concentrate upon Him there would be a matrix, or rather a mold, formed in the psychic world reaching up through the planes into His world. He would use this as a channel and come through it to manifest upon earth to men.

"The *Sugmad* is part of every *tuza*. He is the sacred faculty in men which is called the creative imagination. This is the divine spark in all *tuzas*—and it is that part which can draw the *Sugmad* down to earth or take the *tuza* up to the *Sugmad*.

"This is the great secret which I give you!"

"The *Sugmad* made all creation and divided up his creative ability with each creature. By doing so, He lost a certain amount of His godly powers, but if He wishes, this power can be regained by withdrawing it from each *tuza*. Yet, to do so, would destroy the *tuza*. This is the only thing which the *tuza* possesses that gives it a divine spark of power.

"Therefore, if you are following me closely, you can see that the *Sugmad* cannot do without His own creation, the *tuza*, nor can the *tuza* do without the *Sugmad*."

"Now the disinterested works are those of the balanced mind. The spiritual seeker becomes indifferent to all things of the life he lives in the physical world. The Zen-Buddhists have a good expression for it: After experiencing the *satori* you die in the flesh and become reawakened in the spirit. For the rest of your physical life on earth you are dead; and when you die life is reawakened.

"You surrender to that divine spark of the *Sugmad* within, and from that moment onward, you are moved by Him, sustained by Him, and dwell in Him. All else has no importance in your life.

"This is the act of non-attachment to which the *Bhagavad-Gita* gives so much emphasis. Lord Krishna tells Arjuna this: 'But the disciplined self, moving among sense objects, with the senses free from attraction and repulsion (interested only as a spectator of the passing show), mastered by the Self (Supreme) he goeth to victory.'

"There are five destructive passions. They are: *Kama, Krodha, Lobha, Moha*, and *Ahankar*.

"First, *Kama*, or lust, is a normal function which may be allowed to run into an abnormal demand. It may include drugs, alcoholic drinks, tobacco, or even

124

foods which are eaten for the sake of their tastes.

"The chief function of *Kama* is to pull man down to the common animal level and keep him there. It obligates man to fix his attention on that which is common to both man and brute.

"It is a principle of psychology that whatever the mind concentrates upon, that thing becomes a part of the individual.

"Second, *Krodha*, is anger. Its action is to stir up strife, cause confusion, and scatter the mind so it cannot concentrate. It destroys peace, engenders hatred, and turns individuals and groups into enemies, only for the purpose of destruction.

"Some of the signs of *Krodha* are slander, evil gossip, backbiting, profanity, fault-finding, jealousy, malice, impatience, resentment, mockery, destructive criticism, and ill will. Anger is mental carcinoma.

"Third, *Lobha*, is greed. The function of greed is to bind us to material things and to cloud the mind to all higher values. It is the most poisonous of all the unholy five passions. As *Kama* binds man to the animal plane, and *Krodha* to the mental plane, so *Lobha* binds man to the mineral plane. It fosters worship for the commerical gods of gold and silver.

"Some of the signs of *Lobha* are miserliness, lying, hypocrisy, perjury, misrepresentation, robbery, bribery, and trickery of all sorts.

"Fourth, *Moha*, is attachment, which means delusive attachment, infatuation. This is the most insidious, the most deceitful of them all. It generally comes with the appearance of well-dressed respectability. It has noble bearing and good credentials. It can announce itself as your ally and friend, and its ideals are plausible.

"*Moha* begins its deadly work under the guise of a most respectable friend. Its method is to blind you to the relative values of your surroundings and associations so that you may begin to set false valuation upon them. After you have become absorbed in them, you will have little time for anything else. This is exactly the purpose of *Moha*. You are kept forever on the go, most of the time between work. *Moha* takes you from your spiritual traveling.

"Hence *Moha* is the king of procrastination. It involves you in everything possible to spend your time on nothing, so you can become a slave to it, become attached to it.

"The main sign of *Moha* is worry, anxieties, and business complications. None of these have any importance in the Far Country, so you shouldn't be bothered with them here.

"Fifth is *Ahankar*, vanity, the last of the deadly five. The word *Ahankar* has two meanings. First, it is the faculty of the mind that gives the power of awareness of the *tuza*, self-differentiation, the I-ness. It is that faculty which executes the mandates of the Buddhi, or the *Sugmad* in the interest of self. But abnormal exaggeration of this faculty becomes the *Ahankar* which is vanity, or self-admiration.

"*Ahankar* has a thousand claws by which to dig into the minds of its victims. Its deadly poison infiltrates the entire being. Beginning generally in infancy, it seldom ceases to operate until death of the body. It can carry on until the *tuza* shakes it off in some manner or enlists the help of a teacher.

"It is the last of the five deadly passions to surrender. Its method is to distort one's viewpoint, to present everything out of proportion, to make itself the center of the world."

"There is no escaping from *Karma*, for once it is created and the debt is incurred, it must be paid. But there is a way of living without creating *Karma*. You know that all living beings in the first three planes of this universe create *Karma* by every act of their lives.

126

Even the *Bhagavad-Gita* says that inactivity itself creates *Karma*, and no one can escape it. But there is always a way of escaping it. What is that way?

"By acting always in the name of the *Sugmad*."

"It is with complete *Vairag* [mental detachment] that one enters into the world of the *Sugmad*. Man must attain this state of being which is like the sun, shining upon all alike, yet asking nothing in return. The *tuza* lives forever by giving, not by receiving.

"This is the grand paradox, not only of all spiritual thought, but of all that Eckankar has to offer. You get most by not wanting anything.

"Conversely, by receiving much you impoverish yourself. By selfish accumulation you become bankrupt. As Emerson, the American philosopher, said, 'you run in your own debt.' For in the long run, you can never get something for nothing. Each piece of coin must be repaid if you don't earn it in the spiritual sense. The law of balance in the spiritual realms is just as inflexible as the law of gravitation. To give and give only, not once thinking of reward, is the beginning of immortality."

"You cannot be bound up with earthly duties and worldly possessions. You take nothing with you into the Far Country but your own inner possessions, which are the qualities that the *Sugmad* has given you from your original birth in time and space.

"One cannot assume the attitude of self-righteousness. This automatically defeats his own purposes and nullifies all progress made. One must keep *Ahankar*, vanity, subdued, and he must allow charity and love of knowledge, power, and strength to have full sway over his thoughts and actions.

"By desire, we are bound to objects of desire. This is why the complete detachment of the mind from every worldly object is necessary if we are to enter upon the path to the Far Country. That detachment avoids bondage to the world and its objects of sense desire. This is why we should not love anything with a desire to possess it. The moment we do, we enter the first stage of slavery. This applies to a family or goods. A detached devotion to a family may not be so easy, but it can be acquired. A detached love is a much higher and nobler sort of love than that which demands possession and self-identification with the object of one's love. When such identification takes place, one is completely lost. He is not himself anymore, and he is less able to even serve the objects of his affections while he is a slave to them."

"Controlling and destroying desires are two different things and, knowing this, man can progress upward along the path to the *Sugmad's* domain.

"Destruction of lower desires can never be done by negation. Yet negation is the method employed by ninety-nine per cent of the human race, by parents, by teachers, by reformers, by the courts. They all forbid things. They tell people what they must not do. They write into their human laws, 'Thou shalt not.' A few understanding ones offer something better to attract the minds of the disobedient. But it would never be done by negation.

"The world rushes madly into a mire of sensation, bondage to work, bondage to pleasures, and bondage to a thousand things. *Karma* kills out all progress of the spiritual traveler, and he sinks into the mud of desires.

"But then the traveler learns of *Bani* [music of the audible life current] and by use of this lifegiving force he becomes a light unto himself, and a light unto others, for he is no longer in bondage to the lower desires."

"There is nothing greater in the eyes of the

Sugmad than the *tuza,* for it is that which holds the divine secret, the sacred imagination which the *Sugmad* wants again for Its own. This is why It calls for all *tuzas* to return to Its place in the far world."

"Beliefs and speculations offer little support for the hope of immortal life. All the elements of the many world religions are of doubtful value for the reason that they are dependent upon ancient books and metaphysical theories. This takes the matter out of the category of knowledge and robs it of its chief value.

"In order to get to the roots of immortality we must look at the basis of the philosophy of Eckankar. It is not a religion, nor a philosophy as known to the scholars of the educational systems in this physical world.

"The sad fact remains that nobody on this lower plane knows anything about the *tuza* or the real man. What are the component parts of him? This question is never answered in the laboratories of the earth world.

"The several parts of man will be a quick study for you, beginning with the lower stratum, which is first of all man, the animal. He is a physical body, called by the Orientals *Isthul Sharir.* He has a body which gets hurt, sick, and which finally dies and returns to the soil.

"There is another man inside the physical body, a much finer body called by the spiritual travelers the *Sukhsham Sharir,* or subtle body, *Nuri Sarup,* or light body. It is commonly called the astral body by the occultists. It makes connections with the outer world.

"When seen by the physical eyes it appears to sparkle with millions of little particles resembling star dust. It takes shape with the character of the individual and has five senses, just as the body in the outer realm. When the physical body dies, this body remains as the instrument of expression on the astral plane.

"Inside the *Nuri Sarup* and quite distinct from it, there is still another body, much finer and more subtle than the astral. It is known as the *Karan Sharir*. This means the causal body, so named because in it is the real cause, or seed, of all that is to ever take place in the individual's life. It is also called *Bij Sharir*, the seed body.

"This body is divided into two or more strata, each of which is given a different name. One is sometimes known as the mental body, because it acts as a sheath around the *tuza* and is very sensitive to impressions from the mind. Its function is to receive and transmit impressions between the mind and *tuza* on one side, and between the mind and astral body on the other.

"A perfect record of every experience the individual has is established in these countless ages of experience. Out of these experiences character is formed and from that character all actions flow.

"The mind body is the fourth unit in the construction of the *tuza*, or rather the man. It is so closely related to the *Karan Sharir* that it is not easy to distinguish between them. The mind body is a sort of sheath covering the *tuza*.

"When reaching the *Daswan Dwar* region, all bodies but the mind body has been shed, because the *tuza* no longer needs them. He can, without any instrument of communication or meditation, know all things and rejoice in all things by direct perception.

"When the *tuza* rises upward from *Daswan Dwar*, it sheds this mental body and becomes itself. It alone has the power of knowing by direct perception. All knowledge opens before it without any sort of instrument.

"The mind itself is sometimes divided into different sections according to the plane on which one is operating. The *Nijmanas,* the inner mind, carries the seeds of all actions within itself. It carries the *sanskaras,* which means impressions of all former lives. Sometimes we speak of the causal mind, the *Sukhsham* mind, and the physical mind, according to the region or plane upon which the mind is operating. But this is only a distinction for convenience.

"Last of all we come to the real man, or *tuza,* the spirit. These two terms we use synonymously. This is the core of being, and it is the fifth unit in the structure of the being that is known as man."

"There has never been a religion founded, a good book written, a good picture painted, a good poem composed, nor a good invention developed, except by going *inside* and concentrating on the task at hand. Even if one is not conscious of the exact thing he is to accomplish, he gets results by concentration. That is the great thing in the process—perfect concentration, becoming oblivious to the outer world of sense and centering attention upon that which is to be found in the Far Country. This is the way of attainment, no matter in what line of endeavor. No matter what one is to achieve, this is the one and only method leading to success. Concentrated attention is the key that unlocks all stores of wisdom, of truth and spirituality."

"Every spiritual traveler keeps a vigilant eye upon his mental processes. When he begins to enter into the inner worlds, even to the slightest degree, he must beware of his own misleading mental creations. In all of his waking consciousness he is to remember that his mind is his worst enemy, as well as his most useful instrument. But the main point is that he must keep it under control every moment. The mind is a useful servant, but a bad master."

"A spiritual darkness broods over this world, and

all men are sick from it. Spiritually, and often physically, the whole of mankind are sick, blind, deaf and dumb and covered with sores. Cancers of moral corruption eat their way into the vitals of the human race.

"The race can change only when it awakens to find that the spiritual travelers are here among them and ready to help any who come unto them. Nobody can make his way very far into the Far Country unless he has the assistance of the spiritual travelers.

"These spiritual travelers know that the path to the Eckankar is the only way to reach the world of the *Sugmad*. They know its dangers and its blessings, and they lead the blind upward along the path until they can see for themselves. The travelers find only the blessings for the followers, bypassing the dangers but always letting their companions know what might befall them if they are careless."

"All that human consciousness classifies as evil is made so by a depletion of spirit. This means darkness, of course, lesser life, lesser light. Man cannot live happily without spirit, and the more he departs from spirit, the more he experiences what to him is evil. As with an individual man, so it is with the worlds themselves. The less spirit substance is in them, the darker they are and the more troubles are experienced by their inhabitants."

"Now I am going to discuss the various yoga systems. It is well that we go over them so you will know those practiced by students in the East. They are interesting, but the spiritual travelers do not need them.

"First, *Hatha Yoga*, which aims at the control of mind and acquirements of the *siddhis*, or what are called psychic powers. This is done chiefly through *asana*, or physical postures and exercises. The *asanas* have beneficial effect on the health and bring control over the senses.

"Second, *Raja Yoga*, which seeks to concentrate and still the mind by ways and natural methods of mental discipline and control. Emphasis here is placed upon the mind, rather than the body.

"Third, *Ashtang Yoga*, is a comprehensive scheme of yoga training. It consists of eight elements, the first five of which—*yama, niyama, asana, pranayama, pratyahara*—all refer to the body. The last three—*dharana, dhyana* and *samadhi*—all refer to the mind. The aim of this yoga is to merge the *tuza* with the *Eckankar*, the universal *tuza*.

"*Pranayama* chiefly consists of breath control, and by that means, the control of the *prana*, plays a very important part in this yoga.

"*Laya Yoga* consists in the absorption of the mind in the astral light. This is generally achieved through the practice of *mudra*, another Hindi name for exercises.

"*Karma Yoga* is the yoga of action. It enjoins its followers the necessity of doing one's duty, whatever that may be, without fear of blame or expectation of rewards. The essence of *Karma Yoga* is the ideal of duty well done.

"*Bhakti Yoga* is the yoga of devotion, and it appeals most of all to people of emotional temperament. It discards all rites and ceremonies and seeks union with the Eckankar through the force of love only.

"*Mantra Yoga* aims at the acquirement of psychic powers and spiritual or astral regions by constant repetition of certain formulas which are supposed to set up particular vibrations, especially when repeated with the mind fixed upon certain centers. The formulas, as such, are believed to have an efficiency of their own.

"*Sahaji Yoga* is what we know as *Surat Shabda*

Yoga, or that yoga of the sound current. This is practiced by the spiritual travelers. It is the oldest yoga system known in the history of mankind.

"It consists mainly in following the inner sound. This is the point which distinguishes the yoga of the spiritual travelers from all other systems. This is the supreme test which must be kept in mind while studying the other systems. If the sound is not a vital part of them, then they are not the system of the great spiritual travelers.

"Many will insist that one system is about as good as another, since all are intended to lead to the same goal. Far from it.

"That teacher who doesn't teach or practice the science of the sound current is not a master of high order. Nor does his system lead to the highest achievements. Every spiritual traveler in all history has taught and practiced the yoga of this life sound. It couldn't be otherwise, for this is the system established by the *Sugmad* through His early spiritual travelers in this lower kingdom.

"Most followers of Indian yoga systems will agree that most, or all, of the old systems are very difficult and require much time, rigid asceticism, and great self-abnegation. The path of the ordinary yogi is a rugged one. But the method of the spiritual travelers is not the way of the yogis; it never has been. Before there was ever a yogi system the science of the spiritual travelers was known and practiced among men. But the exact methods of the travelers has from time to time become obscured, or even lost, in times when real travelers were few or unknown to the general public. Then yogis developed methods of their own, trying to substitute for the path of the travelers. The two systems then have been running along parallel courses for centuries. But not only are the methods of the yogis different from that of the saints, but their final objective is different.

"Most of the yogis, even the best of them, know of nothing beyond the astral plane, commonly termed the *Turkya Pad*, with the possible exception of a very few who may have reached the *Brahm Lok*.

"Here they are automatically stopped, unless they have a spiritual traveler who, himself, goes further. Stopping there, most of them believe they have reached the supreme heights. There they accept the *Brahm* of that region as the Supreme God of all.

"But the travelers go so far above and beyond *Brahm Lok* that when they reach that region they have only fairly begun their journeys upward. While most of the yogis and imperfect travelers believe *Brahm* is the supreme authority, the travelers know that he is only subordinate in the grand hierarchy of the universe. While the OM of the *Vedas* and the *Gita* is regarded as the most sacred word in all Hindu philosophy, it is because they believe it to be the sound symbol of the supreme being. The travelers know that it belongs to one of the lower lords, who is not above the regions of *Awagawan*—of death and birth.

"He is still under the law of *Karma*, and is, therefore, liable to fall into the snares of *maya*, becoming a mere man again, or even going lower than that.

"The yoga of the travelers accomplishes that which the yoga of the Vedantists can never do. It is therefore vastly more efficient and, moreover, it has been adapted to the needs of modern man. This is its most beneficial effect.

"It is what the person of this world calls modern in method, and yet it meets all the requirements of all ages. In every age of the world, the travelers have used a system exactly suited to the needs of that people and the times. People change, to some extent, from age to age, and so the travelers give them in each age exactly that system of yoga which is best suited to their requirement.

135

"But the yogis hold on to their archaic systems which are now quite out of date, wholly unsuited to the average man of this age. The nervous constitution of the modern man is somewhat different from that of the men of ten thousand years ago. The yoga of the travelers may now be practiced not only by the ascetics, but by all men in all walks and conditions of life, while carrying on their routine duties at home. This makes it a universal system of spiritual science for all under any condition."

"Immediately when one dies on this plane, he or she is taken by the messengers of death to the subtle regions where *Dharam Raya*, the righteous judge, sits enthroned to judge every individual according to his rewards.

"The Christians call these messengers of death, the Angels of Death, or the Dark Angels, for dark indeed they are. In India they are called *Yama dutas*, or the messengers of Yama, the King of the Dead. This judge is always in court to take care of all comers. There is no waiting, or sitting in some jail cell.

"No one ever questions the judgment. No comments are made, no oratory is presented for the defense, no pretended righteous condemnation is given by the prosecution. The prisoner himself makes no complaint and asks no favors. He understands that he is to receive judgment and asks no help for he must consent to the judgment. That is the law of the *Sugmad* from the highest to the lowest world.

"He is taken to that region, or condition, where he has earned his place, be it good or bad. He will remain there for a fixed time, according to the judgment just rendered and handed down to him. After that period has expired, he is then returned to this world, or some other world, to begin life anew.

"This is the routine procedure. He may enjoy a rest in some heaven, or paradise, some pleasant country perhaps many times more beautiful and delightful than any portion of this world. There he may remain for a year, a hundred years, or perhaps several thousand years, all depending upon his *Karma*. The higher he goes, the longer the period of his residence there.

"If one's life has been that of a lower order, he may be taken to some purgatory, or reformatory, often called a hell, to endure the punishment earned by him during his lifetime. He cannot escape. He must meet the appropriate punishments. But there is one feature about all such punishments that must be understood: They are remedial and not vindictive. They are intended for his good, to produce a reformation of character, but they are not eternal as man is often led to believe, especially in the Christian religion. But the law is inexorable. Each one must get just what he has earned and just what is needed to impress upon his inmost consciousness that he must obey the laws of nature or be punished.

"After his period of discipline is over on the subtle planes, he may be required to re-enter earth life in some lower form, to finish his *Karmic* schooling."

"There is in this greater universe an almost endless series of sets of dimensions, one above the other, like our three-dimensional world in which we live here, reaching up to the highest worlds. Each set is separated from the one just above it by the differences in the substances, the fineness or coarseness of particle, and the different rates of vibration.

"These differences make one set invisible to people living in another set, because the eyes of people inhabiting one region will have a limited range of vision, making it impossible for them to see a region much above or much below their own region. This is the reason we cannot see the astral worlds by, or through, the physical eyes.

"But with the astral eyes we can see on that plane just as well as we can see on the physical plane with the physical eyes. So it is with the still higher worlds. With each higher world, or set of dimensions, the light and the beauty increase materially, as does the happiness of the inhabitants.

"At the sublime moment when the traveler steps out into the higher world, he begins to realize that he has acquired vast increase of powers, as well as joy. It appears to him, and it is a fact, too, that he can do almost anything he wishes to do. Not only has he increased his powers, but his knowledge and understanding have expanded proportionately.

"At this time, the whole material universe appears as an open book to him, and all dark mysteries have vanished. In other words, he finds himself in possession of all knowledge of these lower worlds. He now knows them and has power over them. From here on up, each world gained gives him complete knowledge and power over the worlds below.

"The traveler is now free to proceed on his way to still higher zones. He may not allow himself to be unduly detained in order to enjoy the new world he has just entered. He must proceed always upward, for there will be no ending of the worlds he is seeking."

"*Chelas* leave their bodies much in the same way a dying man leaves his shell, except the neophyte does it voluntarily and the process is always under his control and he can come back into the body any moment he wishes to return. Otherwise, his passing out of this body is practically the same as that of the dying man. He thus learns how to use the *shottama*, understands what death means, and views what lies beyond death. He may even become acquainted with the astral home to which he is to go when he finally takes leave of his physical body. He may also converse with friends and family who have long before left their physical bodies.

"This achievement cannot fail to interest the neophyte, since it solves the gravest problems of life and destiny. It is one phase of the great work of the spiritual travelers. They have broken the seal of death, and so to them and their charges there is no more death. All of this is positive knowledge, not speculation or guess work. Neither is it the interpretation of any book.

"All the world, the Western world in particular, has been accustomed to think that no man knows, or can know, what lies beyond the portals of death. Some assert, with apparent finality, that death lands the soul upon some mystic shore from whence no traveler ever returns. Of course, a few assume that death ends the individual career of a man. It is time, however, for men to cease to think of death in such gloomy moods. In fact, there is no death at all. There is simply a shifting of the scenes, an awakening in a new world."

"After one is able to leave the body voluntarily, there is not only no death for him, in the ordinary sense of some dreadful catastrophe, but there is not even a moment of unconsciousness or a shadow of darkness. One using the *shottama* energy steps out of his body at will and in full possession of all of his faculties. He knows exactly what he is doing, and he remains always in full control of the process.

"Of course the spiritual travelers leave their bodies when the time comes for them to go. However, when that time comes, they go as they always have, only now they sever all connections with the body and discard it. They simply step out of their bodies and go, as one would step out of a close, stuffy room into a beautiful garden.

"When the spiritual traveler leaves the physical plane, he goes where he wishes, for he is the traveler of all higher regions. If he pauses on the astral plane, he uses his astral body there. If he goes up to the causal plane, he functions there in his causal body. If he goes up to the third plane, he discards all bodies and from there up he acts as free spirit, unlimited and unhindered. As pure spirit he knows all things by direct perception, without any sort of instrument of contact, such as he was obliged to use on all the lower planes.

"A dying man, of course, breaks all connection with his body when he leaves it; but the spiritual traveler, when he leaves the body as a part of his daily work, leaves a sort of connection with it, so that he may return to it at will. The Bible speaks poetically of this connection as 'the silver cord.'

"This cord is never broken by a spiritual traveler, or his neophyte, until they are ready to leave the body for all time. Then they, of their own will, break the silver cord and pass on up to perfect freedom. This is all there is to that much-dreaded thing men call death."

"Spirituality is caught, not taught. Once one has learned the secrets of spirituality at the feet of a traveler and has been enlivened with the life impulses received from him, it is no longer essential to be in constant physical association with him. The *chela* can have inner association with the traveler anywhere and everywhere."

"Man is a god clothed in rags. He is a master of the universe going about begging a crust of bread. He is a king prostrated before his own servants, a prisoner walled in by his own ignorance. He could be free. He has only to walk out of his self-constructed prison, for none holds him but himself.

"The spiritual traveler has always to contend with three powerful obstacles to reach his goal, each of which has been almost insurmountable. These three are monarchism, priestcraft, and popular ignorance. Slowly and steadily the traveler has been forced to fight every step of his way against these three.

"Religion is supposed to be a friend of man, and yet they have been in deadly conflict during nearly the entire period of history.

"Priestcraft is now almost an absurd anachronism. It still exists everywhere in strength, but someday it will disappear from the face of the earth.

"Ignorance is also gaining, despite the schools and the work of many who are trying to educate the old and young; but they are going at it in the wrong manner, not in the form of showing man how to get out of the body.

"All that physical science knows is that life manifests in certain ways. It follows certain well-attested laws. Scientists do not even try to guess the ultimate causes of life. Only the travelers, having access to the higher planes of being where the phenomena of both mind and spirit can be seen by them, know that without mind and spirit both, no life can manifest on this physical plane, or on any plane where matter is a factor in such manifestation.

"Scientists do not admit that the assumption of mind and spirit animates nature. But this is no assumption to the travelers, for they can see it working from the higher planes down to this earth."

"So many men find it difficult to believe in the spiritual travelers, because they are not common among people. One of the strangest freaks of the human mind is its tendency to discredit all modern things, especially those relating to religion, and to give emphasis and glory to that which is ancient. Modern mind cannot accept that which is right before its eyes, but it will swallow instantly that which was written in a book two or three thousand years ago.

"Modern mind cannot believe in the living spiritual travelers; but it finds no difficulty at all in accepting the story of some adept who lived in the dim and distant past. That men should ever have developed the strange notion that all mastership and all revelation of truth should belong to the past ages is one of the anomalies of history. It is one of the most unfortunate.

"The fact that great spiritual travelers have lived with us for centuries on earth and are here today is one of the most important, the most cheerful, and the most hopeful thoughts that man can have. The light of the spiritual travelers is in no way dimmed by comparison with those of the ancient past—in fact, many of the ancient masters are still living with us here on the earth world."

"Without imagination man remains a creature of the earthdust, a materialistic thing. Man either goes forward in his imagination or remains a prisoner of his senses. He is free to soar like the birds or remain upon this earth as a reptile and make his home within the dirt."

"Wisdom is the highest quality which the *tuza* can develop within himself. Once he has wisdom then all things are possible, for he knows where and how to find all things of life, and all his desires in the lower worlds are forgotten. He no longer wishes for anything, for it is foolish to do so."

"Man is the highest form of creation on this plane, and he is only a sojourner here. The wisdom that he learns in his material existence is only a speck compared to that in the innumerable worlds of light and sound beyond.

"Wisdom, as the mother of all good, can guide him into these worlds, provided he listens to her. Power is his source of motion, and his instrument in which to gain that divine energy which controls all life on any plane in the Far Country. Freedom is that liberation from all obstacles and the opportunity to live a full life in the spiritual worlds.

"Wisdom also goes with a good mind, purity, and perfection. Power goes with the supreme will, manifested in all worlds and in creativity. Freedom goes with immortality and single-minded devotion to the cause of the *Sugmad.*"

10. Questions and Answers on Eckankar

In this conversation, I asked Paul Twitchell to discuss the concepts, literature, and history of Eckankar.

"Just what is the basic principle of Eckankar?"

"The basic principle of Eckankar, the ancient science of soul travel, often called the science of total awareness, is that the world of creation is finished and that the original of all things lie within man.

"Therefore, the way by which each person can regain the original mastership of his own 'Garden of Eden' is by use of the faculty of imagination, with which the *Sugmad* [God] has endowed each of us as His divine gift to all men.

"Eckankar teaches that we can have solace in the higher states of consciousness and in soul-travel experiences, such as those which were common in the lives of the old Christian saints and the lives of the Eastern adepts."

"Why is soul travel, or getting out of the physical body, such an important part of Eckankar?"

"Man must someday leave his fleshly temple anyway, so he should learn by going in and out of the body that he can give it up at physical death without suffering."

"If I study Eckankar, will you send me the formulas and secret knowledge that I need to be able to do all the amazing things that you can do?"

"The knowledge of Eckankar is not hidden, nor

can it be distilled into a pat formula or something which can be read from a book. The knowledge of Eckankar lies in a process which the neophyte slowly develops and prepares for himself. The *chela* does not acquire the power, but rather he becomes a part of it. Neither does he accept the power, because it accepts him.

"In my advanced study of spiritual knowledge, I have learned that after a man has passed a certain point, he cannot go back. There is a point at which he becomes dedicated. He reaches this point and passes it on his journey to the *Sugmad*. But before the dedication comes, the *chela* must be purged of all weaknesses; he must break all petty restrictions.

"All those who strive to reach perfection in this life will follow a path similar to the one which I have described in my own experiences. A teacher, guru, or an adept, from the other worlds or from this one, will appear at the time when the *chela* reaches a certain period of his spiritual life. The period of schooling is difficult, but it is well worth the struggle to have such an adept as Rebazar Tarzs accept one as student on the pathways of that Far Country."

"Is there any scripture, or holy book, in Eckankar?"

"The *Shariyat Ki Sugmad (The Way of the Eternal)* is the ancient scripture of the path of Eckankar. This book is the oldest of its kind known on the planet Earth. It is said to have been known in the antediluvian world and back into the hoary years of those so-called mythical nations we know as Lemuria and Atlantis. Only two monasteries in Tibet have any of these writings in their keeping.

"Eckankar has remained closer to its original form than any of the philosophical or religious teachings of today. However, Eckankar is neither religion, philosophy, nor metaphysics, for it is a path to God.

"According to our tradition, the *Shariyat Ki Sugmad* has been handed down by word of mouth

145

from Rama, the first known world savior, who came out of the deep forests of Northern Europe and traveled across to Persia, where he paused long enough to give those secret teachings to a few mystics, whose descendants were to become the followers of Zoroaster, the Persian sage. Rama then proceeded to India, where he settled and taught that man could have the experience of God in his own lifetime.

"No written instructions were ever put down for the followers of Eckankar until about the sixteenth century, when Kabir, the Hindu mystic-poet, took it upon himself to unwrap the mysteries of the ancient science of soul travel.

"The *Shariyat Ki Sugmad* consists of fifteen chapters, each about thirty thousand words, made up of cantos, or what we would call verses in dialogue form, wherein the *Sugmad* speaks to His chief disciple, Sat Nam. The *Sugmad* utters statements of the highest spiritual nature to show that He wants all souls to be lifted into the heavenly realm again. For example, He says, 'I am eternal, therefore I am free. All who come unto Me shall experience the freedom of eternity'; 'Freedom is a completeness within itself, for soul must enter into the divine light or suffer the effects of the lower reality'; 'The true reality is spirit in any universe of Mine, and he who looks upon it as giving him existence and experience is indeed a wise man.' "

"*Does Eckankar have a creed? Christianity, for example, has the Apostles' Creed, the Nicene Creed, and the Athanansian Creed. These are each an authoritative summary of religious belief to be professed by the adherents of Christianity.*"

"The ancient creed of Eckankar is this: 'All life flows from *Sugmad* downward to the worlds below; nothing can exist without the ECK [cosmic current] which can be heard as sound and seen as light.

146

Therefore it is necessary for man always to be aware of the sounds of the ECK and to see the *Nuri* [light] of the *Sugmad* in order to live within the highest spiritual realm.'

"As one studies and practices to reach the higher worlds, he gradually comes to the realization that all life is sound and light flowing out of the Godhead through himself. As he grows more aware of this, he comes into God-realization, and sees that the source of this sound and light, which is within himself, is only a part of that universal sound and light flowing from above. When he realizes this and accepts the *Sugmad* as that source, his life will become greater in every respect."

"*Are the spiritual travelers to be compared to saints, who act as intermediaries between God and man?*"

"The spiritual travelers refuse to consider themselves as intermediaries between the Universal Mind and man. Of course, they are the agents of God, but they will not allow anyone to rely upon them as a support. The purpose in Eckankar is to teach every man to take his own responsibility and to stand upon his own spiritual feet, anywhere, at any time."

"*You keep emphasizing the concept of freedom in Eckankar. Why is this so important to you?*"

"The essential nature of Eckankar is freedom from all things—the complete independence of soul. Soul is the central reality of the individual. Soul, being a happy entity, will not be controlled by anything other than the Holy Spirit. Thus we must devote ourselves to the practical work of our daily lives and try to realize the guidance of spirit in every affair. This depends on our maintaining a non-attached attitude. The moment we start creating special points, ideas, and distinctions, we exile ourselves from the state of God-consciousness and miss the infinite freedom of reality.

"This philosophy of nothingness is not a pretense. One must become aware that pure freedom is the essential law of God. Such freedom is never conceived: It lives. But it only comes alive when all concepts cease. We do not revolt against dogma and beliefs, but we allow soul to become the impersonal channel of the Holy Spirit, which uses soul to uplift the world of matter. We know the difference between being awake and being asleep, between light and darkness, and between freedom and slavery. There can be no half-way for the traveler. The passage from one state to the other constitutes a spiritual transmutation."

"What is this 'God-realization' to which you so often refer?"

"God-realization is often sudden, unexpected, and spontaneous. When the mind gives up its inner tension, this experience of light and sound comes pouring into soul like a violent flood. It lifts us into the heights of the True Kingdom and snaps us out of the sleep state into the consciousness of awareness. We are now alive, and at once become the mouthpiece of truth. The whole secret of our power lies not in the fact that we have the secret of power, but of life itself."

PART II*

*11.   Love Is the Foundation
        of Life*

Love is the profound current of life! Everything
has its center in love on every existing plane!

The spiritual science is based upon love, but not
the love we know in this world sphere. It is not even
that love which we seek for the bliss of God!

This latter love is an illusion of the mind. This love
is said to be the highest love of all. But this is not
true. The God-love, or the love of all, is not the
highest love of man!

Many who have come to this earth to teach man
have left the conception of God to be worshipped in
many different forms. It, as we might designate the
God-reality, is not a law, a principle, a man nor a
being, nor the stream of life which flows through
every living organism in the living worlds.

All of this is abstract. We go further back than
that. We go to the complete fountainhead of that
stream of life permeating all the planes of existence.
Out of this current flows the great stream of atoms to
give us the total substance of consciousness.

This is the source of all—the absolute! This is
where we dispense with all, and face the great reality.
The name we give to this deity in Eckankar is the

*Author's note: The first part of this book, through interviews and
documents, has given the reader an introduction to Paul Twitchell—the
man, his life, his work. In the following presentation, I have let Sri Paulj
speak for himself.

Sugmad. Nameless in form and ideal is this great ruler of the seventh plane world, and all the universes. He controls all, gives life to every living atom that moves through the millions of worlds. All is under this magnificent soul. His voice is the living word. His body is the light of the worlds!

Then we come to the question. Whom or what do we love, as humans?

Do we love profoundly the great soul, the *Sugmad?* I tell you, yes. But we cannot love Him as the *Sugmad,* for this is too great a strain on the minds of those who have hardly gone past the astral world, and even for those who have reached the mental plane. It staggers the human mind, not yet trained in the universal concepts of the spiritual science.

So we draw the lines finer to what we must love. We will tighten our understanding to bring the conception to two aspects of the *Sugmad.* These are light and sound. These twofold elements of the great deity are manifested in the highest state on earth by the form of the living master.

I pause here to say that not all teachers of the truth are masters. There are evolutions of teachers who eventually become masters. The masters will evolve to saints and after this become angels or heavenly spirits and ultimately emerge into the body of the seventh plane deity or remain in His presence. Eventually, if they so desire, they return to the spiritual stream of life as the highest form of consciousness which is taken into the consciousness of a being somewhere, be it on a planet other than the Earth.

For your knowledge, the graduated masters, if you wish to use this term, for identification, often go to other planets like Clarion, Venus, or those where higher evolved souls are living, to help carry on the work of God throughout the universe. Hence, we can think and believe in the flying saucers or other phenomena from the other worlds.

Light and sound, the basic elements in the body of the *Sugmad*, are put into a single ideal and called God for the sake of those without imagination or the hope of knowing God. This is what we love at this stage of our development. Call it God, reality, or the *Sugmad*—anything for the sake of identification. Light is the conveyor of the Word. Breaking this up into an example of what we are trying to grasp simply means that the light is the reflection of the universal atoms, and the sound is the movement of those atoms.

The stream of atoms passing out of the Supreme Being is one great force of positive atoms. But after passing into the lower worlds, below the second grand division, it breaks into two streams, the positive and negative, for these are needed to keep balance in the lower worlds.

The seeker must look for a master, the incarnation of the Supreme Being, or a Satguru, one who has reached the top of the second grand division, and invoke help. He must receive instruction from one of these supreme guides as to the manner of his devotion and procedure to love God.

Now we have learned what to love and that we need instructions to learn to love. Next, we must know how to live in order to love.

This comes through the balance of the attitude toward love. Since we dwell constantly in the great streams of life, we must be taught to balance ourselves within these wonderful spiritual currents. Man cannot escape the negative forces in this life as well as the positive, so we must make the effort of having a well-adjusted mental balance in order to travel the middle path.

Hence the teachings of the great masters of the world who are neither fanatics nor weaklings but strong-willed in God, seeing their own weaknesses and strength; pitting and balancing good and evil in their lives in the two streams of consciousness flowing through their inner worlds.

Buddha portrayed this wonderful teaching to mankind. Travel the middle path, says he.

So, herein, on the middle path where light and sound are so prevalent to him who tries, the consciousness of man eventually becomes the impersonal atom of pure intelligence, and the seeker is no longer himself.

His consciousness is no longer the angry cascading stream of negativism, but in pure balance with both streams like some broad placid river. The usual phrases which tormented his mind are gone, and in their place are serene thoughts that come floating through the consciousness.

It is this special attitude of balancing the mind, in meditation, to dwell upon the twofold aspect of the great deity, light and sound, that shows man where love can be placed. For light and sound is the master within. Therefore the living master is a symbol of the greater One, and to love the inner master is the highest form of all love.

When man can do this he is no longer a bird in a cage of negativism but rises out of that current into the positive stream of life, and balances his consciousness, of the inner self, while living out his life span on earth.

This is the clue of the meaning of true love, and what it is that man should love.

12. Our Modern Confusion in Spiritual Affairs

The subject of religion, philosophy, metaphysics, and occultism seems to be on a rampage among the peoples of the world in our times.

Truthfully there has never been a more confused state of spiritual affairs.

The problem of spirituality which is the overall effect of religion, philosophy, metaphysics, and occultism, is that no two writers, or two teachers, hardly ever agree upon any point. There are two reasons for this: first, everyone fits knowledge to his own state of consciousness; second, because of the difference of semantics which exists in the language of the whole of spiritual subjects.

Strange as it may sound, we all have the tendency to fit any teachings to our spiritual understanding; thus a person with a lack of knowledge may reject the highest teachings because he doesn't understand. Christ was not accepted by everybody. This is generally the fate of anyone who tries to break new ground in the spiritual field.

So much of the essentials of the spiritual works come from the East, and with it brings the confusion of various wording of phenomena and aspects when Oriental terms are used. But once we sweep away the brush then the concept of the terms become clear. For example, that reality we know as God in Anglo-Saxon language has thousands of names in foreign tongues, e.g., *Brahm* in Hinduism, *Allah* by the Moslems, *Sat Nam* by many of the various sects in India and *Sugmad* by those who follow the path of Eckankar. Other names are *Akal, Anami, Sat Purusha, Hari Ray* and *Amma,* to name a few more. No wonder there is so much confusion.

We must not be perplexed by words and symbols. We must go to the heart of all things in order to understand the Divine Reality and Its principle of creation and survival. If we do not do this, then, frankly, one will continue to wander about until the hardships of life will force him into looking for the center of the creation of all things. Until he does, this wandering will be a suffering for the individual.

This means that anyone interested in any subject of the spiritual realm must certainly be very careful of how much he reads, studies, and participates in meditation, for the simple reason that once he goes beyond a certain point there is no return. It's like flying a plane from Tokyo to San Francisco: when it crosses a certain longitude and latitude the pilot must keep going toward his final destination, for now he has crossed the point of no return.

This raises the thought that now we are confronted with the problem of what is going to happen to that individual who has crossed this invisible line, and moved into the inner realms of the spiritual worlds. Under a competent teacher he is taken care of, but with a teacher who has no experience in the work he is liable to get into areas of trouble.

An example of such troubles can be that too much study of any spiritual works, too much participation in meditation and reading leads to lifting the vibrations of the person. If his vibrations are lifted, and are not under any control of himself, or someone who is trying to help, it means that he may become opened as a channel for Spirit, and this divine power flowing through him can come through at too strong a vibratory rate.

It means the power has to go somewhere, and like a highly charged electrical bolt it will attack the weakest part of the body. Troubles begin with health, with other forms of material problems, and the individual affected is greatly puzzled by this phenomena, but doesn't understand what is going on inside himself. So he continues to put the pressure on for study, practice and meditation, and often prayer to get out of this situation. But the stronger he does this, the greater become his problems.

Some teachers rationalize this with the fact that he is serving out a *Karma*, or that troubles always come with a person who goes into the field of spirituality. Granted that the two reasons are somewhat correct, but they are not always the complete basis for his troubles. Any teacher worth his salt in this field should be able to help the *chela* gradually unfold so that Spirit flows through his follower gently giving him the proper benefits of both spiritual and material help.

The guru must slow down the vibrations of the *chela* when they have become too strong. He must keep control of the *chela's* spiritual actions until the latter is able to fend for himself.

One must be prudent in whatever he does in the field of spirituality for it is a different life from that he lives here within this earth world; and his out-of-the-body awareness will often be of a different nature than he ever expected.

Truth is actually an individual process of consciousness. It depends upon the individual how much he, himself, is going to know and learn of it.

13.   Who Says God Is Dead?

The raging debate over God's death has certainly caused a schism between those who claim his demise and those who steadfastly argue that it isn't possible.

Although it has turned out to be little more than a fad for many who follow the thesis that God is dead, there is a strong element of truth in the statement, which we shall see later in this discussion.

Our problem here is that we are somewhat concerned with semantics: the two powers, those of the negative and spiritual forces, and three major states of consciousness.

These three major states of consciousness that we are interested in and which we are constantly dealing with are the human state of consciousness, the self-realization state of consciousness, and God-consciousness. Once we find ourselves able to exert self-recognition according to these states, we know ourselves and can recognize God Itself.

First in this discussion we must take a look at the mechanics of Spirit. Spirit is divided into two aspects, first pure Spirit, which has its home in the God-worlds, above the fifth plane of the invisible worlds. This is the dividing line between the two grand divisions of the lower worlds and the upper worlds. The negative power, often called the psychic force, or universal mind power, has its abode in the lower worlds. This includes the physical plane.

When any person takes up the path to God in a

serious manner, the spiritual power from the upper worlds enters into his human state of consciousness to purify this area of consciousness. But the negative power starts a fight to keep it away from its own field of activity.

We can easily call this the perennial battlefield, and no man is without it as long as he lives in the human body. It is discussed quite well in the *Bhagavad-Gita* in the dialogue that takes place between Krishna and Arjuna.

While in the human state of consciousness we experience pain, anger, doubt, fear, vanity, pride, greed, and other nonsurvival factors of the lower consciousness.

If Spirit is at all successful in overcoming the negativism within this human state of consciousness, soul can move into the higher level we call the fifth plane, or the self-realization state of consciousness.

By movement into the self-realization state of consciousness we have reached the fifth plane of the spiritual worlds, where we have freedom, liberation from all in the lower worlds. We gain perception of knowing who we are, where we are going, and what our mission is here on earth.

This is only a state of spiritual being, gained by soul travel through the lower planes to the fifth plane where liberation is granted and soul returns to the physical body for temporary living, until the body reaches the end of its life here on the physical plane by natural means or otherwise, which is not of the individual's own doing.

From the self-realized state, then, soul moves into the God-realization consciousness where it dwells in total awareness. It knows all things, can see all things and is a part of that we know as God.

When one functions in the total-awareness state while living in the physical body, he does so in the soul consciousness only. He does not have to travel in this state since there is no time and space concepts involved.

While he dwells in the lower worlds in the *Atma sarup* (soul form), he is in space and time and must be concerned with these concepts for traveling.

This explanation had to be given, for it is concerned with the arguments that are flying around about the demise of God.

We must have a criterion by which we can judge the actions of those who are putting up such arguments on either side of the issue at stake.

The whole argument can be summed up in a few words: The existence of God is only proven to those who live in the higher consciousness.

14. The Danger of Resisting the Spirit of God

Resistance to the Holy Spirit is what brings so many difficulties to the seekers of Truth. Belief in their own lack of understanding, which does not see truth in either a partial or whole state, is that which gives added *Karma* to anyone who puts himself in the position of not realizing the difference between the states of human consciousness and God-realization.

It is one of the peculiarities of life that man in his egotistic self does not recognize the fact that when he commits an overt or covert act against anyone who is high on the spiritual scale that he is resisting the Holy Spirit. Thus the results of his act will return to him swiftly. The teacher, guru, master, or spiritual traveler, who acts as an instrument through which the Holy Spirit flows outwardly, is not concerned with what the culprit does for there is no resistance to any hostility toward himself. Therefore the action has no place to go and thus becomes reaction, and boomerangs on the sender so swiftly that he is likely to be amazed at what has happened to himself.

An example of this is the case of the murderers of St. Thomas à Becket, the martyred archbishop of Canterbury, who was in 1170 the victim of King Henry II. The four knights who carried out the assassination of St. Thomas à Becket received the dire punishment of the Holy Spirit. Using the consciousness of the Pope, It forced them to give up their properties and fight in the Holy Land for the Cross, a hard sentence indeed for proud men, for they were captured by the Saracens and forced to live like lepers for the remainder of their lives.

This is an extreme example of what happens when anyone resists or destroys a channel of the Holy Spirit. History does not record what happened to those who condemned Christ and those who carried out the orders of His crucifixion. But we do know that Pilate, who was responsible for shifting the decision to the mob for His death, served out the rest of his life in a state of madness.

Judas committed the grave error of betraying Christ for thirty pieces of silver, and gave up his own life by hanging. One cannot sell or betray a channel of the Holy Spirit for materialistic means.

The slightest act against any channel of God comes back swiftly to the doer. This is true even when one gossips and uses malicious talk about God-realized people. Personal examples can be given here about those who do not understand the nature of anyone who dwells in the higher consciousness, and the troubles that befell them when they attempted to belittle or ridicule the teachings of the blessed channels of God.

The greatest evidence here is that you see the spiritualized ones rise higher, and the maligners go down the survival scale in spirit attitude until they have a loss of spiritual and worldly goods.

This is not magic in any form which punishes the culprit and gives benefits to the spiritualized ones. No, indeed, but only the working of the Holy Spirit through the consciousness of those who are willing to let it use them as a channel. This is the danger that the maligner of spirit is up against; for spirit turns away any overt act that is done against its own channel and returns it to the sender. It acts as a protection against the enemies who try to attack its own instruments.

George Fox, founder of Quakerism, gives a long list of what happened to those who persecuted him during his earthly ministry. The list is long and impressive. It should serve as a warning to those who are guilty of such deeds. But man in his human state of consciousness is not impressed and continues to make grave errors that cost him agony, difficulties, and more *Karmic* debts.

Since the cosmic spirit is a law unto itself, it has the power of returning to the sender whatever he might be sending to the holy essence of life. Thus the spirit of God, in the lower world, works in a dualistic manner; it can curse the sender or it can bless him. It depends on whatever communication the sender wishes to establish with a person well versed in the spiritual nature of God-knowledge.

Whoever keeps a record of such happenings will find that the law of spirit is exacting in its demands for payment. This is actually *Karma* on a much higher level, for when anyone holds a hostile attitude toward a holy person it creates a *Karmic* debt which must be paid off. Even though the impact may be stunning and one of shock, the *Karma* is worked off at once. But often it will stay with the individual who has created the debt for many years.

My own casebooks show a large number of incidents which happened over the past years to those who attempted to make attacks on my person. I also saw what happened to several persons who felt above the spiritual law in trying to malign Sudar Singh, a high spiritual teacher, my first master, and a member of the ancient order of the *Vairagi* adepts of India.

Please remember that the person who is dwelling in the cosmic state of consciousness is not responsible for whatever happens to the sender of malignant thoughts or words. He is protected by an armor of light, and the attacker is actually the responsible party and the victim of his own makings.

There is an old spiritual law which must be alluded to here: "No harm can come to anyone unless we so desire it to." In other words, when we open our consciousness to harm it will become a part of ourselves and bring injury into our lives. But under the protection of the spirit nothing can injure us in any manner whatsoever.

Therefore we must remember that when we seek to avenge our feelings in some manner or other we are putting ourselves under the law of retribution. To seek to balance the scales of spiritual justice by human effort only creates confusion, nothing more. The belief in human justice is no guarantee of success to right the wrong. Only the Spirit of God can do that.

Resistance to spirit brings only confusion, unhappiness and disillusion in this world. The stubborn mind is a burden to the carrier of it, but the one who is nonresistant to spirit and welcomes spirit into his life lives in joy and happiness.

15. The Importance of God-Realization

Often I have spoken out strongly against the idea set down by metaphysicians for the last few hundred years that we should seek wisdom first, *instead* of God-realization!

It is spiritual law that we must first seek the Kingdom of God, which is God-realization. There is little need to seek His attributes, like love, wisdom, and understanding, for they are secondary causes and will be attained provided we have first the enlightenment of Divine Reality.

Although Christ emphasized this quest as spiritual law, somehow man has become sidetracked. It was during His great Sermon on the Mount that He urged all, "Seek first the Kingdom of Heaven and all else will be added unto you!" Thereafter, he re-emphasized the spiritual law of God-realization as the primary goal of one's life in practically every public speech. It was the one point He tried to pound home to all who had ears to listen.

Unless we have been trained from childhood to seek God-enlightenment first, it is extremely hard to develop this habit of understanding, but one never need be discouraged in seeking God, the reality.

Here is the difference between the God-consciousness we seek and human-consciousness. In the human state of consciousness, the lower, we are concerned with thousands of desires—to have healing for health, to manifest more money, to get the right mate for love and understanding, and more desires than can be listed here. The problem arising here is that the metaphysicians in the past have pampered our greed and emphasized the idea that God gives us anything we desire. It is a dishonest approach to solving problems of people in trouble. This approach has caused dire distress to many and it never fulfills the wishes of those seeking ways out of trouble. Most reports of failure to the teacher brings a standard reply, which puts the guilt upon the student, thus introverting him and making him an emotional and mental cripple.

The truth about this is shocking. God is not interested in the human consciousness, but only in the continuation of life. He is vitally interested in trying to get human consciousness opened for spirit to flow through to the outer world of matter, energy, space, and time. He knows all things that go on in his worlds, including the chirp of the cricket, but He is not interested in the problems which human consciousness makes for itself. It is left up to us to find the solution to the state of affairs in which we live on this plane. It is not difficult to resolve all problems, provided we allow ourselves to follow the spiritual law and not be diverted by those who seem to be ignorant of it.

We must seek the Kingdom of Heaven through our own consciousness. This is the only path. This is the position from which the man Jesus spoke as the Christ, and it is the same state in which each of us must establish ourselves. When we do, we, too, speak from the Christ-consciousness for we are living in the God-realized state.

This means that one must spiritualize his consciousness in order to establish himself within this state of God-realization. He must reverse the lower attitude to the higher. This is done by keeping the mind constantly on God and by doing every action and deed in His name. The Orientals personalize this state of being by electing someone in the flesh as dwelling in God constantly. They recognize him as representative of the God-force, or the channel through which the Holy Spirit flows in abundant blessings. He is supposedly the Son of God, the Christ, Ancient One, and the Buddha. He wears given titles such as *Sat Guru*, the *Sri Maharaj*, *Babji*, and the Supreme Master. The idea is not completely true, for each of us can become the channel of Holy Spirit which can flow with supreme abundance to all. The misconception lies in the fact that the Orientals select one individual to be representative of the clear channel for the God-power, on which they depend to give them blessings instead of seeking it for themselves. The spiritual law, however, clearly says that we must each personally seek to become a clear channel through which the Holy Spirit can flow to the outer world.

We should not give worship to anyone in the flesh as many do in the Orient. Respect for attaining the God-illumination is correct, but not to the extent of worship, for it is our mission here to establish ourselves in this state of high consciousness. We are individually the supreme consciousness of itself, and if we are equal to it, then we have not recognized this fact. The moment we do, then we have assumed the role of living in it. It is not someplace else, but here and now always. We can help to put ourselves there by chanting some sacred word or scriptural verse, silently or aloud, which is preferred, and performing all actions in the name of God, without the expectation of reward. Once we put ourselves in this state of consciousness, we have found the Kingdom of Heaven.

16.   Spiritual Realization Can Solve
Your Difficulties

In the field of spiritual affairs we find many teachings in the mind sciences and many religious teachings that are promising material and spiritual rewards through different methods—especially, resolving difficulties.

However, we find that the practitioner of most methods which consist of the manipulation of thought will come to grief after periods of practice for any length of time.

First, he will start thinking that there is something wrong with himself and this will create a guilt pattern which will push him downward on the survival scale into grief and apathy. He becomes a victim of frustration and defeat.

The other thought is that there is something wrong with the system of such teachings which are supposed to lead him to many gains through practice of these methods. This leads him to running from teacher to teacher, and trying to examine dozens of systems. Sometimes he is guilty of taking two or more courses from different institutions and reading as many books as he can possibly put his hands on in the subject of gaining material and spiritual rewards through mental and religious sciences.

While there is nothing basically wrong with manipulation of thought to gain a material reward, one must remember that he gets what he goes after; and often it is something that is not wanted when the goal is achieved. Also seeking parts of the whole instead of the whole which puts the parts together is wrong.

Unless one seeks spiritual realization first, he is apt to fail at all material and spiritual goals which he has set for himself. So many fail to understand this and remain in one pattern of thinking throughout their whole life. Just before the ending of their existence here, they admit they were colossal failures in the methods they were trying.

When anyone starts out to solve his problems either materially or spiritually in this way, he is doomed to failure. He may for a little while find himself doing well, but in time he will come to the end of the good cycle and find gigantic obstacles blocking his way. A few can be successful at manipulating the psychic energies to gain success in solving problems, the vast majority are not.

For some strange reason we have been told for many years that God is willing to reward us for spending time in meditation or trying to use various methods of the imaginative processes to resolve problems. But this is not true, for we cannot begin to be successful until we have started reaching the field of the universal worlds—that which is sometimes called the Kingdom of God.

Christ reiterated this many times throughout the Gospels by his words "Seek ye first the Kingdom of Heaven." His Sermon on the Mount is a classic in laying down the basic spiritual law that says we have to have spiritual realization before all things come to us in a natural way.

No one who has lived on earth in the human consciousness has ever been successful at resolving problems. Not even the many saviors and savants who have trod among us found the psychic to be the ultimate way. They found that problems can only be controlled and never resolved in this physical world.

But we must dwell in the spiritual consciousness before true success begins to come to us.

We cannot manage our worldly difficulties successfully unless soul is able to live again in the spiritual consciousness of itself. In seeking this state of established experience we must first seek self-recognition—what we call self-realization.

The practitioner does not go anywhere, does not seek, nor does he experience anything but recognition of himself. The more that he practices the art of self-recognition the greater becomes his awareness of the God-state of realization.

There is no progress or development but rather unfoldment. It is looking deeply into one's self constantly. This is not introversion which meditation often leads us into, but it is having an objective viewpoint about ourselves.

This is the difference between Eckankar and many of the other systems of seeking this God-state. ECK uses the simple technique of self-recognition which is sometimes called contemplation; while yoga and other systems use heavy meditation.

Contemplation can be streamlined to the simple explanation of being completely interested in a subject whether we are sitting at a desk working, or in silence. Meditation means a sharp one-pointedness of concentration for long periods.

Westerners are not suited to the meditation methods of the Oriental religions. Our hurried daily pace does not allow us to have time for heavy concentration and long periods of silence outside our jobs. Most of us are not geared for this inner seeking.

Anyone who spends over one-half hour in silence without gaining results should stop and wait until later to make another try. Generally the span of attention will not hold any longer than this, and then the mind will begin to jump like a monkey.

Too often the writer who has laid down rules for

anyone to follow is a professional in the spiritual field, in a manner of speaking, while those who are reading his works are amateurs, or beginners. When they cannot master what he has taught, they feel that something is wrong with themselves, for it seems that anyone can follow his instructions.

This is not at all true. The reader or student must find that the system must fit himself, instead of his fitting the system. If he does not find the system fitting himself, then it should be discontinued and he should find another one which will.

However, no system will give as complete success as one which shows him how to enter into the Kingdom of Heaven—the spiritual consciousness—and live there through self-recognition.

17. Freedom From Death

Freedom of soul is possible in this lifetime. The freedom we seek, called *Jivan Mukti*, is that which is liberation from the Wheel of the Eighty-four. This is the Wheel of Transmigration, that which brings us the ills of this life, or any life that we live here upon this world plane.

By entering into the stream of spirit we are liberated from the atrocious Wheel of the Eighty-four; that of the birthing and dying of the physical body into which soul must be born until it learns that its home is not in these lower worlds but in heaven. The connecting up with the cosmic stream of life is the assistance which any spiritual traveler will give to his *chela*. It ends his suffering here in the physical body and turns his attention toward the heavenly worlds.

Unless the *chela* finds a teacher in the living flesh, who can work with him inwardly as well as outwardly, then he has wasted his efforts in trying to reach the worlds of pure spirit. He will also find this exists on every plane in the lower worlds. It is the teacher whom we are following from the point of contact in the physical realm who can take us through the lower worlds into the worlds of spirit. Hence the outer and inner teacher is this one who has made contact with us to assist in getting the proper aid.

All groups in the religious and philosophical fields who are trying to put their *chelas* into the stream of life—the cosmic spirit—will have the problem of having a living teacher. Those sects that depend upon ascended masters in the invisible only, do not find the true path; they are acting as learners and will all their life depend upon something that is not practical and will find these invisible masters could fail them. Thus, we find the outer teacher is not the completion of the whole, but the inner teacher is the true master. He will not fail you where all others will. His chief responsibility is to link up soul with this stream of life, making the cosmic spirit a part of ourselves, so that we will be freed of all suffering and reincarnating into the physical life.

By doing this the *chela* achieves self-realization. He comes to know who he is and how this knowledge can affect all his life. He will find new values and once he has made the change from looking outwardly at the material things of life, then he accepts the spiritual existence of himself in the worlds of the Divine Reality. Actually the cosmic spirit takes over and guides his life into paths far more beneficial than before, for both soul and body. He is now on his way to God-realization because of this initiation, or linkup, with cosmic spirit.

Once this happens we can see through the illusions of all that surrounds us. We will find that most writings on the subjects of religion and philosophy are hardly more than dialectic fiction, and really not sacred scriptures. Once we are connected with the stream of life, the cosmic spirit, then we are actually on the path to God. We are not concerned with the imagination, for it is dropped on the astral plane. Problems are a worldly illusion and we cannot accept them, but since the illusions are with us, we then take control of them.

This is the *Jivan Mukti*, the liberation of soul, or the birth of the Christ Child within one, as many want to call it. Once this divine spark takes hold it grows into maturity within soul, and we are the living examples of the Divine Life itself. Rising to higher planes liberates soul from all human ills, as mounting the sky in an airplane relieves one from the effort of walking. Therefore, the teacher is the light of the world, for he brings spirit, or light, with him. If one centers his attention on this light and walks in it, there can be no darkness in him. If the *chela* opens the gates of light within himself, as he is urged to do, he walks unobstructed into the Kingdom of God. He does this only by the light of the living teacher, who passes it on to him.

Christ told Nicodemus, a Pharisee, and ruler of his sect, "Except that man be born again he cannot see the Kingdom of God." It means that we must be brought to light, from darkness, from ignorance to enlightenment, from blindness into sight, by the action of the cosmic spirit within each of us. It is one of the basic principles of life that all teachers will try to pass on to all who come into their orbit of vigilance.

Thus death becomes the last great illusion to overcome. The liberated soul steps out of the body, at the end of its physical journey, as if casting off an old cloak. Death simply vanishes into the mist of life, as we move along the normal course of spiritual development, learning to leave the body voluntarily and travel in the higher worlds. By entering into the planes of spiritual light while in full consciousness, all illusion of death will disappear. So the word, or spirit, will abide in the *chela*, as much as his consciousness is expanded to accept it. It will also grow in us only to the extent of how much we expand the consciousness to allow it to have growth.

It is this, the all-purifying spiritual current, that brings new life to us, allowing us to gain spiritually and reach the heavenly worlds. It is the supreme cleansing agent of all worlds and the creative force that lifts each of us into the true worlds of God.

Seeking it, obtaining it, is the only practical purpose of life. It is our true mission to have the experience of *Jivan Mukti*, the perfect liberation of soul here and now.

18. The Eck-Vidya—
The Akasa Science of Prophecy

Prophecy is perhaps the oldest arcane science in the world. It is accepted by billions of people throughout the world who have depended on it since the dawn of time through ESP, spirit mediums, clairvoyants, astrology, and oracles.

However, few have ever heard of ECK-Vidya, the Akasa science of prophecy, which is the *modus operandi* of delving into the future used by the adepts of the path of Eckankar, the art of soul travel.

ECK-Vidya is much more inclusive than astrology or any of the mystical arts that are utilized by the well-known ancient and modern prophets of psychic precognition. It uses more Siddhi powers than the practitioners of prognosis have ever dreamed could be possible.

The art of ECK-Vidya is only an aspect of ECK, which is the fulfillment of the total awareness with God. Prophecy, or foreseeing events before they happen, and *déjà-vu* for seeing what has already happened, is on a far wider panorama than any of the lower arts of prophecy.

ECK-Vidya can foretell the deeper and more subtle events of life, including that of any individual, even to the all-inclusive prophecy of a minute-by-minute mental or physical action to take place in one's life.

ECK is only a path to God, but in its own broad framework are included thirty or more kinds of facets, e.g., prophecy, healing, self-realization, making events for one's own future, and a large number of other things too numerous to deal with in any one book. All of these powers are carried on upon such a high level that those of the occult, metaphysical, and religionist teachings can hardly follow. The vibrations of anyone practicing ECK-Vidya are so high that those on the lower spiritual scales can never be compared with them.

The ancient mysteries were established upon the keystone of prediction. The Elysian, Orphesian, Pythagorean and many other ancient mystery schools had initiations which consisted of the chief priest going into trance and giving predictions for those receiving instruction into their particular cult.

The foundation of the argument against Socrates during his trial was that he was giving the youth of Athens false hope by predicting the political and material future of individual persons and of the chief Greek city.

The most famous of all mystery cults in ancient times was the oracle of Delphi in the Temple of Apollo at Delphi. During a visit to this famous oracle, which is now one of the great tourist sights of ancient ruins, I met a man who claimed that the oracle still speaks to those who have the gift of prophecy and divine insight. At first I took his words lightly until I sat alone on the great pile of ruins near the mouth of the oracle.

Its words came slowly and distinctly. When the first shock of surprise had passed, and I had slowly digested what had been said, it was clear that the ancient gods of Greece still lived for those who had the ears to listen. Shortly afterwards I began the practice of ECK-Vidya.

The shrine of Dionysius, which is also located on the island of Delos, was another of the great sites of ancient prophecy. However, an oracle which was still active up until the early part of this century was hidden deep in the wild mountain ranges of northern Tibet. It was known as the Voice of Akivasha and was located at a craggy, unexplored site known as Tirmer. I visited the oracle twice with Rebazar Tarzs, once when I was initiated into the ancient order of the Eck adepts, and at another time when I wished to confirm some of the prophecies of my mission in this life.

The oracle was one of the oldest on this planet and was used until about fifty years ago by the ECK masters when initiating *chelas* into their order.

Very few use the hoary *modus operandi* of giving prophecy for those who wish to know their future, via the ECK-Vidya method. The old instructions of divination which were handed down by oral teaching is gone. Those Tibetan masters who were able to use the ECK-Vidya way of looking into the future have dwindled into a handful, headed mainly by Fubbi Quantz, the Abbot of the Katsupari Monastery near the old site of the Voice of Akivasha at Tirmer.

The ECK-Vidya method of reading the Akasa records is not simple, but it can be learned. The *chela* places himself in the care and under the tutelage of an ECK guru, trusting in him implicitly and following his instructions to the letter. By constant meditation in the various drills given by the master, coupled with strong spiritual shocks, the *chela* is able to awaken the *Tisra Til*, the spiritual eye, and bring about the release of the *Atma Sarup*, the soul body, from the physical body, putting it above the realm of time and space.

Here one is able to view the whole area of the individual time tracks of himself or of any others in whom he may be interested.

This action leads the *Atma Sarup* upward, into, and through the other planes until he has reached the culminating experience of *Moksha* or *Samadhi*—that which we know in the West as cosmic consciousness, or "entering into the Kingdom of Heaven." This same state is known in the circles of the ECK adepts as the Eckshar.

When at this position, the top of the ladder, one knows his future and the future of others if he so desires. He is also able to envision the forthcoming events for the world races, including disasters, individually and collectively.

Generally, one does not induce the trance state to leave the body, but this can be accomplished by what is known among ECK adepts as the *Saguna Sati*. We would know it as instant projection, the ability to move at will out of the body into any of the higher states of consciousness.

I can do this by simply concentrating on a physical object for a few seconds while repeating the secret name of God. There is usually a ping within my head, but it often sounds loud as a mortar gun. I find myself hovering above that area we know as time and space, looking at what might be in store for anyone who has requested knowledge of his future.

Few know the mechanics of how the *Saguna Sati* works; but the formula is there, and if used as directed, we find that the future can be read. Predictions that I have made in the past seem to have come true. For example, two years ago when all the psychics and mediums were announcing that an earthquake would sink the Southern California coast, I dismissed it as erroneous. The date passed and we are still above the sea. Predictions which did come to pass were those which foresaw the dumping of Kruschchev, the downfall of Nkrumah, the kidnapping of Tshombe, the Middle East crisis, several major air disasters, and dozens of other important predictions gained through the ECK-Vidya methods.

Eck-Vidya actually means total knowledge. All that comes to him who can read the Akasa records, via the soul body, is that which is known as divine cognition. This is given to the reader by the Holy Spirit, the essence that flows out of the principal source, the Heavenly Kingdom, into the worlds below, making contact with whatever soul is in conscious awareness of it and is making an effort to contact it in this awareness state.

Most persons close out this direct contact with the Divine Spirit, and even though it is working within them, their physical senses fail to open to the inspiration of this relationship with God.

This is why we say that illusion is the mother of negative power. The lower world force throws up deceptions and diversions so we will have our attention focused on its illusion rather than on the spiritual cognitions of the divine Holy Power.

The practice of the ECK-Vidya has nothing to do with the practice of yoga, spiritualism, drugs, Vedanta, astrology, and any kind of Oriental rituals. We are not concerned with the *asanas* (postures), *mantrams* (chants and vibrations), *mudras* (gestures and binds), and *pranayama* (breath control). Neither does ECK-Vidya have any relationship with the study of the *Kundalini* and the *chakras* of the yoga practices. In fact, yoga is considered to be too much effort, and the lifting of the *Kundalini* is a task not worthy of its exertion.

ECK-Vidya works on the principle that the world is an interlocking unity which can be observed once we lift ourselves above the regions of time and space. Within this position we are able to see all as a totality, and all that is needed is a concentrated effort in one direction, to sort out the powerful magnetic fields around those whom we are reading. Once this is done, we start reading their Akashic records.

One can be in the midst of a group of people and still put himself into the state of higher consciousness without being the least suspected. The physical body will continue to function as usual, walking, talking, sitting, working, eating, drinking. The physical senses will be registering what the soul body is looking at while in this out-of-body state.

However, the goal of ECK is not to develop the acquisition of *Siddhis* (supernormal powers) of this nature. ECK-Vidya is only one aspect of the broad path to God.

Generally speaking, ECK-Vidya is the achievement of spiritual insight which will enable one to look into his own future, as well as that of others, on a minute by minute basis or a day by day reading, as it is applied to economics, health, and other important, but personal, matters.

This is the realization of the great works of Divine Deity which can be applied to all things and to all events which we meet in the everyday routine of living.

One should never be side-tracked from the ultimate realization with God. Our values change as our recognition of the inner strength and relationship to God occurs.

The ECK-Vidya is only in part the experience that we call "cosmic consciousness."

19. The Cat That Could Do Out-Of-Body Projection

Jadoo was a half-Siamese, silky, black, lady cat, whose intelligence and psychic abilities, including out-of-the-body projection, could equal any *homo sapiens* with definite talents in this field.

Since her demise years ago she has always been around for a true reason, besides having an affection and devotion for me. She twice saved my life.

When news came that she had lost all her nine lives she was aboard a foreign ship, the *Southfall*, which sailed under a Danish flag while en route to Cape Town, South Africa.

She appeared in her astral body, over a distance of thousands of miles, to announce that she had made the passing over into the other world. She gave her little whistle that made her so different from other cats, and rubbed against my leg to show that she was thinking of me at the last moment. But as a matter of fact she has not left me at all.

In her physical life Jadoo had more adventures than Marco Polo during his famous travels. She was the delight of a small boy's life in a small river town in the deep South.

Yet in her astral life she has stayed with me and given me all the affection of an earthly pet. Once she aroused me from a deep sleep to warn of the dangers of an overheated stove that would have exploded in minutes.

At the time I was living on a houseboat on Lake Union, near Seattle, Washington. Jadoo had passed on many years before, but she had come back in the astral body to keep me company in those bachelor days.

On another occasion Jadoo was responsible for letting me know that somebody was lying in wait with the intention of robbing me.

Several years ago when I lived in Washington, D.C., I was returning home from a late evening engagement. I had parked the car several blocks from my apartment and was walking home when Jadoo suddenly appeared and blocked my way. A few tiny whistles and mews proved that something was wrong. She wouldn't let me pass, but forced me to take a side street. Nearing the apartment building I saw what she was doing, for a man was running up the street toward me from a corner where the lights were dim. If I had gone the regular way, he would have committed robbery. I got into the apartment building just in time, thanks to Jadoo's help.

Jadoo is visible at times, but more frequently she is apt to lie beside me on the couch, and she often rubs against my legs. Many times she has wakened me by hopping on the bed and curling against my feet for a night's sleep.

I do not see her in many cases, but I feel the impact of her weight alighting on the bed and her fur against my flesh. All evidence shows that she is around constantly.

Jadoo is recognized by the whistle for which she was famous as a world-traveled cat, a sort of tinny sound that is similar to those penny whistles kids used to get as prizes from Cracker Jack boxes.

It was this sound that often frightened people who used to visit. They could not understand what it was, nor did I try to explain, for the explanation would have seemed so silly that it would have appeared that I was off my rocker.

Her whistle was created by a harelip Jadoo had in her physical life. She had always made this goofy, little whistle at ships as they passed the tugboat in the New Orleans harbor where she had lived before I inherited her.

Cats usually have little use for water except for that found in goldfish bowls. But Jadoo loved the sea more than Moby Dick or Captain Bligh. Sometimes I felt that she would have been a good navigator if that harelip had crooked another way for vocal sounds.

Everybody on the New Orleans waterfront knew Jadoo. Captain Jeffry had picked her off a South American banana boat from a crew member. For a little while she lived aboard his tug for it had lots of sea motion going down the delta to pick up ships heading for the Crescent City.

She could signal the approach of a steamer entering the port of New Orleans by the way she would try to imitate the ship's whistle with her own tinny, little sound. Jadoo was acquainted with all the shipping line vessels by just the sound of their whistles.

During a trip one summer to New Orleans, on the *Delta Queen*, a Mississippi river packet, I inherited Jadoo from the old tugboat captain. It was a delightful gift for a boy to have a world-traveling cat that could also whistle.

She became a fast friend when she learned that I was willing to take her on voyages. Our first trip together was a cruise to Port-au-Prince, Haiti, where I went to study Voodooism for awhile. We shipped everywhere possible to continue my studies in the spiritual and religious fields, although at times I had to earn our board and keep across the sea to some foreign port and back again.

Though it is generally an unwritten law among

seafaring men that animals are not allowed aboard ships, Jadoo was given special privileges. She provided a certain amount of relief from the monotony of being at sea with her silly whistling and antics.

I soon learned, however, that Jadoo could do out-of-body projection. Often when in port a few of the crew members and I would go ashore for a few hours liberty and Jadoo would make an appearance and follow us everywhere. Then I found out that Jadoo had been also with the other crew members left aboard the ship. Jadoo was being in two places at the same time.

After a while it became common to witness this sort of phenomenon. When I was traveling in the other planes she often accompanied me, as if just for a lark.

Finally I returned home to the small Southern town on the Mississippi where only an occasional riverboat put in for repairs or to deliver heavy equipment and oil. I probably lingered ashore too long for her.

One day Jadoo disappeared. I heard later that she had gone back to sea, probably because, in her estimation, riverboats were small potatoes for whistling at, and landlubbers much too tame.

Occasionally Jadoo would appear in her astral body to let me know that all was well. Word would come back from somebody who had seen her aboard a tramp steamer in some foreign port. Then came the evening when she came back astrally to announce that all of her nine lives had been used up, and that she would be hereafter in astral heaven.

Jadoo was buried at sea with full honors, which was deserving of her independence and love of the sea.

It was, I thought, the closing of the book on Jadoo's worldly life. But recently, in a change of residence to a remote waterfront place where the surf pounds heavily day and night, a solid black, half-Siamese female was sitting on the breakwater staring at Gail and me. It has become friendly and it hangs around the house quite frequently. Can this cat be Jadoo reincarnated?

It is the second time this has happened in the past few years. Earlier, several years ago, when living on the waterfront in Seattle, a similar black cat appeared from out of nowhere and stayed at the house for months then disappeared as quietly as she had come.

20.   The Role of Dreams and Sleep

During the sleep process, there is a rebalancing of chemicals, life forces, and a general readjustment, not only to the physical body, but to the various spiritual bodies of man. Most spiritual teachers, and those seeking the higher truths, live on such a high level of understanding, so in tune with the cosmic spirit, that they can operate on a work level for nineteen or twenty hours a day and not be fatigued. Three or four hours of sleep is all that is necessary for them. They live a full life, yet work on a relaxed level. They do not carry the burdens of mental strain, but have long since learned to cast their load into the cosmic stream of spirit and rest in God.

Let us consider the dream level. Many persons dream vividly and in full color with every perception fully aware of what is taking place. Others dream in black and white and then with only a few senses of the dream experience. Some place great importance on the nature of the dream and keep a daily log to see if there is connection between the dream and the waking state, as J.W. Dunne did with his experiment with time.

It is true; there is a connection between the dream state and the waking state, for the dream is put together from the materials taken during the waking state. Dreams are often a part of the subconscious memories and need careful analysis and understanding. Literal interpretations are of little value in the majority of cases. But when one is out of the body, working above time, as Dunne so aptly did, then we have a case for new understanding and prediction, as well as the gain of divine knowledge.

The sensual type of dream was emphasized in the studies of Freud. It has little to do with sex, but it is the pleasurable dream connected mainly with anything that gives pleasure to the body, including eating and drinking.

Second is the projection dream, which is the type known and studied in the mystery schools. It is the type of dream which is due to the forces, spirits, and teachers of individuals having the dreams. Any teacher or guide can teach us in the dream state. He also takes the individual into the other worlds to study in the Temples of Golden Wisdom, so the *chela* can eventually get enough knowledge to be on his own.

The third type of dream is the memory dream. It consists primarily of past lives. This type shows us *Karma* now in our life and tells us why we are here. If you wish this experience, make a postulate that you are going to dream of a certain period in history on the past time track which concerns your past lives. You will likely have the dream.

Fourth is the spiritual dream. It consists of precognition, soul projection, and clairvoyance. It opens the future time track so we can see into it. We remove the space-time concept and enter into the warp of space-time to see what is happening. This type of dream was used by the old Biblical prophets to mark the future for their people. We can see our future through dreams and change it accordingly.

When we can dream and be conscious of the process, then we have become the dream master, and we can see that the waking state is only a dream state. Just as we can learn to manipulate the environment in the dream state, doing what we desire, simply knowing that it can be done, so it can be done in the wakened state, when we know how. Once we accept the fact that we are going to dream consciously, we can learn to be in charge of our dreams and have a knowledge that we are dreaming. We can change the events, move at will, and change our dreams if we so desire. Eventually we become the master of any dimensional experiences.

The only reason we are in this particular environment is that we have agreed at the moment that it is solid and real.

21. The Longevity of the Ancient Adepts

One of the great mysteries of history is the report of the longevity of the mystics hidden deep in the Himalayan mountains along the Tibetan border.

Rebazar Tarzs, the great Tibetan spiritual master, who is the torchbearer for Eckankar, the venerable science of total awareness, or soul travel, is said by many to be well over five hundred years old in his physical body.

He looks to be a man of about thirty-five, almost six feet tall, and he walks with a springy stride. A maroon-colored robe covers his muscular one hundred and eighty-five pound frame. His eyes are coal black; his hair is clipped to about a one-inch length; and his beard is trimmed to the same length. Both are as black as his eyes.

He is one of the spiritual masters in the descending line of the ECK gurus who have inherited the hieratic responsibilities for this planet, especially for those seeking the way to God through Eckankar.

Practically everybody living in the physical body desires to be like Rebazar Tarzs, free from pain, disease, and old age. It is an aspiration which grows with the passing years, and as our ambitions fade on all other things, it becomes a consuming desire. We want to give up all things within the human realm and become like these ancient adepts who have lived far beyond the normal span of life.

In examining history for accounts of those spiritual giants who have dwelled among us, we find its pages filled with examples. St. Anthony of the Desert, who lived during the fourth century in the Egyptian desert as an ascetic, is reported to have passed the one hundred and fifty year mark in his physical body. As he lay dying, St. Anthony requested his companion, a junior in years (only ninety-seven!) to fetch his shawl, which was at a monastery fifteen miles away. This request was fulfilled by the aged friend, who ran thirty miles so his master could have some warmth during his last earthly moments.

Most of us who long for a lengthy life of this nature seldom think of the responsibilities that go with longevity. For example, the adepts of the Vairagi order, sometimes called the order of the ECK masters, who are chiefly located in the spiritual city of Agam Des, in the remote wilds of the Himalayas, have the tremendous task of working with the uplifting of the human race on this planet and other planet worlds as well.

Rebazar Tarzs has lived but one life in one body. But he is only one of the youngest in the line of the ECK masters. Many of these adepts are using the same body they were born into many centuries ago. Some have such longevity that we cannot believe it possible when in their presence. All of them are men and women who seem still to be in the prime of their physical and mental lives.

This is certainly true of those who have reached a degree of spirituality and who have learned the laws of God. Longevity is a well-known fact to anyone who is capable of doing soul travel, because he is in control of the physical body and its various pressures. He has become a Pinda master and had gained the ability to handle any problem on the physical plane which might confront the body and its senses and the environment into which he has placed himself.

The story of the longevity of St. John the Apostle is one of the most interesting accounts in our spiritual records. Nothing has been left to give us an account of his death, but there are many detailed stories about the expirations of the other disciples of Christ preserved by the Christian Church.

Little has been said of St. John after he wrote the Revelations on the Isle of Patmos, but reports show that he was living during the Middle Ages in a fabulous Kingdom in the East under the name of Prester John. This would have made him about one thousand years old.

Having gained a certain amount of ability to be an extension of consciousness beyond the Pinda stage, we find that when the awareness is placed on the soul plane and can operate from here, we are able to do many things never before understood and, seemingly, of a fantastic nature. We have now become what is known as the *Atma* master.

Surely we know then that the Wandering Jew, who was commanded by Christ to remain on earth in the physical body until He returned, must have become a Pinda master. There can hardly be any doubt about this. He has gone through many transformations, always renewing himself to serve new concepts of physical deathlessness, but always trapped within the realm of the matter world.

These adepts in the ancient order of ECK have reached greater heights than the *Atma* plane. They are proficient in running a physical body while operating on another level. The physical body goes on about its daily routine as if there is nothing at all different in its usual affairs. These are the ECK masters whom we often call the spiritual travelers.

We find that many of those who are able to do out-of-the-body travel live to a ripe old age, although they do not stay here as long as the spiritual travelers who are keeping their bodies intact for specific reasons.

190

Among those who were able to live in their physical bodies beyond the average age and keep it in a healthy state were: Nanak Guru, who was said to have been over a hundred and twenty-five before he finally passed away; Sudar Singh, who was reported to have been approximately a hundred and five at the time of his death; the old Chinese master Suto T'sing, who was reported to have lived for two hundred and sixty-seven years in the same body. Fubbi Quantz, one of the ECK masters, who is head of the Katsupari monastery in the remote Tibetan mountains, is said to be several centuries old, much older than Rebazar Tarzs. The list could go on indefinitely.

These ancient ones learned the art of keeping good health through projection, which is one of the distinctive features of ECK. But it does not mean that we are all going to live like the Green Robe monks of the Andes, or as long as those masters of the Far East that Baird Spalding spoke about in his famous series, *The Lives and Teachings of the Masters of the Far East.*

Since so many who have learned to accomplish the extension of consciousness into higher states have proved that longevity is possible, we find that it is a fascinating study. We find that soul travel can be used for self-healing, as well as for aiding others, and that it will take us into the world of good health, prosperity, and long life. Not many of us, however, are going to become like the ancient adepts whose bodies last for centuries, simply because we have no purpose in living this long.

The reason that we wear this physical body for only a few score years is due to our *Karmic* debt. Unless we have disposed of it, we must go from body to body in various incarnations. The next logical factor is that the human race has limited itself in thought form to living out a single life in a short span of years. Neither do we learn to control the body so

191

that it becomes immune to disease and harm. We are not apt to think of ourselves as going beyond the normal age span, as did old Thomas Parr, the eighteenth-century Englishman, who lived for one hundred and fifty years with vigor and vitality.

Should we be fortunate enough to learn the art of rejuvenation, such as the *Ayur Vedha*, a system of renewing body health, our physical age can be reduced to at least make us look and feel thirty years younger. The *Kaya Kalp* treatment, which is used for bringing back youth and health, is given in the Katsupari Monastery in Tibet by the ECK master Fubbi Quantz.

There are other systems utilized throughout the world which also have proven to be very successful in regaining youth and health. The only trouble is that most of them are so well hidden that we hardly hear of them. They are, of course, much easier to follow than the famed drills of the *Eshwar Khanewale*, or what we know in English as "the God-eaters."

These are the ancient adepts of the ECK masters who live in the spiritual city of Agam Des, near the wild border of northeast India. Some have used their physical bodies for several thousand years and would put the aged citizenry of Hunza down as babes-in-arms. They are able to consume the cosmic spirit for food, which preserves their bodies. Among the Christian saints who could do this was St. Catherine of Sienna.

Heading this order of ECK masters is Yaubl Sacabi, whose age is beyond human conception. The old men who lived as a group in a rural area of middle England during the eighteenth century and defied nature by living out their one hundred and thirty-five year life spans, seem mere infants compared to some of the ECK masters.

Madame Blavatsky, who founded the Theosophical Society, made the world acquainted with the masters of the White Brotherhood. Koot Hooni, leader of these masters, and many others of those in the White Brotherhood, have records of having lived for many centuries. But it is suspected that the line of ECK masters have outlived most of them.

Babaji, the founder of the Yagoda Satsang Society, which is known in the Occidental world as Self-Realization Fellowship, is said to be several hundred years old. The only purpose of his long life in a physical body is to continue the work of Kriya Yoga. This is the same reason that Rebazar Tarzs keeps his own body as an ECK master—to serve the world and the human race by elevating all to the higher spiritual life.

If we can come to this degree of high realization during our life here, to selflessly serve humanity and its spiritual needs, it stands to reason that we can be purified through God-realization.

22.   The Seven Temples
of Golden Wisdom

The ancient temples of Golden Wisdom are often the object of discussions by many who are seeking spiritual truths. But so much of this talk is based on hearsay that legends and myths have grown up about them.

However, those who have had the opportunity to visit any of these magnificent archives of true wisdom will establish the authenticity of their existence.

The seven Temples of Golden Wisdom are gathering places for those who travel consciously or unknowingly during sleep. They are usually taken by a spiritual traveler to one of these fountains of knowledge to gather esoteric wisdom.

Many of the spiritual travelers and teachers who formerly lived and served their apprenticeship in the lower world have established themselves on the various planes in these ancient temples of wisdom, to teach those souls that visit these places.

These temples are located in the following places and under the guidance of the adept so named:

The Katsupari Monastery is in northern Tibet. This Temple of Golden Wisdom is under the leadership of Fubbi Quantz, the famed teacher of the sacred scriptures of the *Shariyat Ki Sugmad (The Way of the Eternal)* and guardian of the first section of these records.

The other school in this physical universe is at Agam Des, the spiritual city in the remote Himalayan mountains. Its name means "inaccessible world." We must go in the soul form to listen and study the wisdoms here. This temple is called the Temple of Gare-Hira, under the master Yaubl Sacabi, the guardian of that part of the *Shariyat Ki Sugmad* which is on the altar of the inner sanctum. Agam Des is the home of the *Eshwar Khanewale* (the God-eaters) for they partake of the cosmic spirit like we do material foods.

Another temple of Wisdom is the House of Moksha in the city of Retz, on Venus. Master Rami Nuri is in charge of it and that part of the *Shariyat Ki Sugmad* placed there.

The School of Wisdom on the astral plane is in the Temple of Askleposis, in the city of Sahasra-Dal-Kanwal. It is under the guidance of Gopal Das, a spiritual traveler in the line of the Eckankar mastership as are all of those who have charge of these wisdom schools.

The Temple of Sakapori is on the causal plane of the other worlds. It is piloted by that master known as Shamus-i-Tabriz, a Sufi master of several hundred years ago on this plane.

On the mental plane is the ancient temple in the city of Mer Kailash. It appears very much like the ancient Temple of Diana which was at the city of Antioch (during the pre-Christian era) where once the science of Eckankar was taught.

Next is the Temple of Wisdom located in the Etheric world, in the city of Arhirit. This is under the charge of Lai Tsi, a high Chinese spiritual traveler in the line of the Eckankar masters, and one of the faultless guardians of the section of the sacred scriptures placed there for the *chelas* who venture this far.

The highest of the golden wisdom schools is that of the Temple of the *Param Akshar* (the house of the imperishable knowledge) on the soul plane. This is the dividing line between the universal mind worlds (the lower regions) and the spiritual worlds (the upper regions of God).

The various parts of the great book of the golden wisdom of God mentioned in this article are parts of the wisdom of the Divine Reality.

The dream method of teaching is one way which those who are looking for truth can visit the various temples. The spiritual traveler will take him out of his physical body nightly, to visit the appropriate plane wherever the *chela* is suited, for his spiritual advancement.

The spiritual travelers named here in charge of the different Temples of Golden Wisdom are masters in the field of the Eckankar line of mastership. Each is capable of the true initiation which is the spiritual duty of any traveler.

These travelers were once inexperienced souls like ourselves, but in the course of their spiritual evolution finally reached the heights of the Divine Reality and became the true *Satguru*, and co-workers with God.

This should give hope to all who enter into the path of God that we know as Eckankar.

23. The Function
of the Spiritual Traveler
in One's Life

It is the duty of the spiritual traveler to see that all who seek his help receive a linkup with the cosmic spirit, so it can use the individual for its own universal purpose.

This divine power, or whatever name you want to give it, has innate intelligence. It knows what we need, and it will furnish us with every good that benefits us for the universal cause. It will not serve a selfish purpose. Hence, if we ask for financial help, spirit may bring health instead, for it sees that without health we would be unable to find the right position or job to give us financial help.

It will not be directed or pushed in any direction. It works on the same free will theory and independence as we do in our own nature. But so many times people will try to demand something of it or attempt to direct it to do something for themselves. It will not reply in any manner, and the person trying this becomes confused, upset, and frustrated.

Those who make a study of Eckankar know that a master will use the power only to assist and lift one into the higher realms of God. Of ourselves we can do nothing, for it is the spirit of the divine power within us that does the work.

Christ told His disciples this at the Feast of the Passover, just before His arrest. Saints, gurus, and all masters, especially those travelers in the line of

Eckankar, are fully aware that they of themselves are helpless without divine power. But once divine power has established itself within us and uses us as a channel of divine communication, it will deal with all our concerns.

So the function of the master is to show those who are seeking God-realization the way toward it. When anyone comes in contact with Eckankar and shows no resistance to these works, it is then that the linkup with the divine power is given him, via the traveler.

The traveler is responsible for seeing that anyone who approaches him to gain truth receives this linkup. It is so subtle that without an outer initiation, often the seeker overlooks it. But he does have the inner initiation via the spiritual senses; maybe in the dream state, or perhaps when the traveler can coax the seeker out of his human state of consciousness into the spiritual state.

Once this initiation has been started then spirit begins to burrow its way through the thickness of the human consciousness much like a drill. Often the reaction of the neophyte is violent, because the human consciousness, or negative state, resists truth entering into it, clearing it for the spiritual consciousness. But spirit is usually gentle in its actions and the change in the individual becomes less noticeable.

However, the heavier the human consciousness is the more violent the reaction might be. This is why the path to God is often called the painful and thorny way. Spirit must clean the individual and collective consciousness of all, so that soul can re-establish its original communication with God.

Life for the neophyte starts getting better in every department, and he gains both materially and spiritually. He is led into the right places for his own welfare. Many times he knows that something is working for him, but he is too busily engaged in the affairs of the objective world to be cognizant of the entire *modus operandi* of spirit.

No master will take over the *Karma* of his students. He knows better, for it would destroy his own health and drive him into despair. But a master can take the *Karma* of anyone and dissolve it by turning the problems over to the cosmic spirit. A master may direct the flow of spiritual power toward a requestee until cosmic spirit takes on the responsibility of either fulfilling or rejecting the request. So many times spirit will fill another need in our life instead of that which we originally requested.

The traveler, then, is the pure channel of God. He has nothing to do with psychic powers. He knows the penalty for abusing these talents, and he is fully cognizant of the fact that only the use of spiritual powers will give him a status in heaven.

The spiritual traveler allows the cosmic spirit to use him and to work through him in behalf of all the world. He often does not know what the results will be, but his needs are always fulfilled by the cosmic spirit.

For example, a few weeks ago when I needed quiet to do some writing on spiritual matters, a bulldozer kept running along the street in front of the house doing repair work. Its noise was disturbing. I asked the driver to go away, but naturally, he did not pay much attention to such a request. It was not but a few minutes, however, before the bulldozer's motor stopped and the driver couldn't get it started again. Just before quitting time, it came alive again, and the driver was able to get it back to its garage. Puzzled and angry at the machine, the driver and the construction people were unable to offer any explanation about what had happened.

Cosmic spirit was taking care of the situation while I was busy doing something for its own cause.

I could give you a hundred or more personal

199

examples of how cosmic spirit works. I have seen it heal incurable problems in health, purse, and human relationships. Once during a debate with someone over the power of God, I casually pointed at a tree in the forest through which we were driving and said, "Look at that tree . . ." but before the sentence could be finished, lightning came out of the sky and split the tree with a mighty crash.

I was almost as surprised as my friend. But spirit needed to prove something to this man, so it used me as a channel to make its point.

Cosmic spirit will lift us into the glorious heights of the heavenly worlds, but it also uplifts and benefits the whole human race whenever we allow ourselves to become the instruments of God. This is our function as spiritual travelers.

24. I Am Always With You

Frequently I am asked what is meant by the phrase, "I am always with you," that is used at the conclusion of my communications. It does have a definite meaning for everybody who is in touch with me, and I will try to explain.

Since the teacher, such as myself, must work with all those who are willing to be with him in studying the science of soul travel, in helping them to connect up with the cosmic power that flows from him to themselves, this means that the cosmic spirit touches the *chela* quickly as he makes contact with the teacher for the first time and will start working out his *Karma* and problems on various planes. In other words the spirit will begin to lift that soul into the higher planes. Many times he will not recognize this fact, but he certainly knows that something is taking place for his own benefit. His mind is clearing, and the material aspects of his life are making gains instead of losses. His spiritual life seems to be progressing, whereas it was at a standstill.

The teacher is the instrument or the hub through which this cosmic spirit flows in a tremendous stream to those around him; it is like a wheel with the teacher stationed at the center and the *chelas* at the rim with the spokes representing the spiritual lines that run from the teacher to each of them. This is the method in which all masters work with their *chelas* and allow the cosmic spirit to pour through themselves via each line to each *chela*. Hence the teacher can be in touch with thousands of *chelas* via his spiritual body, whereas his physical self is working on a plane of limitation. In speaking in the universal language, this means that I am always with my *chelas* in the *Atma Sarup* (soul body), no matter where they might be and what they might be doing.

You will find that all masters who know their spiritual ABC's of divine knowledge speak in the universal language. They talk from the inner planes, and not with the physical senses. It can be pointed out that Christ said, "Lo, I am always with you." He was saying in the spiritual language that He, as spirit, could always be with His followers at any time, any place, whether it was on the physical plane or the inner ones. Buddha, Pythagoras, Apollonius, Mithra, Zoroaster and others who were true teachers of the universal knowledge, said in essence the same thing. They were speaking from the inner planes and not of the physical self, which their disciples were viewing with the outer eyes.

So it means that whenever anyone starts the study of Eckankar, a specific spiritual line is established between himself in spirit and the *Atma Sarup* of myself. Therefore, we are within the circle, and all people who are dwelling in it can be taught the inner knowledge by the master, as they would be via the telephone. The teacher establishes himself with the *chela* the moment he comes into the works, and is able to be seen on the inner planes as well as the outer. The *chela* cannot be passive, and he must bring a certain amount of receptivity to the teachings.

The teacher begins to teach the *chela* via the inner way as well as the outer. He is available on the physical plane for instruction and answers to satisfy the *chela's* mental quests. Not all teachings and replies are given on this outer plane, for the master must use the illuminated way of the inner planes to reach the *chela* because he is more receptive here.

First, we know the teaching comes via the dream state, but as the *chela* starts receiving more and becomes open for the sacred knowledge, he can be taught consciously through the inner via the master's inner form and directions. Eventually he will be able to make contact with spirit itself, and establish himself in the realm of divine reality.

Hence we use the expression, "seek first the Kingdom of God," because in the beginning we are in need of the higher knowledge. It comes to the *chela* because Spirit is the essence of the Divine Source and wishes to use him as a channel. Therefore the right teacher is needed who can teach on the inner way as well as the outer. I give the outer teaching through the voice and writings. But in the other planes it is given by the inner form of myself, working with the cosmic spirit, appearing to all concerned or giving it by impressions for those who are yet unable to see the inner form. All is done by the spiritual lines that flow between the *chela* and myself.

The true universal message cannot be given by a physical channel in its pure state, but it can be when working through the *Atma Sarup*, with the spirit bodies of others. This is essential to all who are studying the spiritual life. We cannot use the outer form and have the outer rituals to reach the higher stages of spiritual development. Nor can we have only the inner and expect to gain all esoteric knowledge and progress. We need both for fulfillment in reaching God.

OTHER BOOKS PUBLISHED BY
ILLUMINATED WAY PRESS

ECKANKAR DICTIONARY
ECKANKAR THE KEY TO SECRET WORLDS
THE FAR COUNTRY
THE TIGERS FANG
THE SHARIYAT-KI-SUGMAD
THE FLUTE OF GOD
HERBS: The Magic Healers
LETTERS TO GAIL
THE ECK-VIDYA, The Ancient Science of Prophecy
THE DRUMS OF ECK
THE WAY OF DHARMA
DIALOGUES WITH THE MASTER
THE SPIRITUAL NOTEBOOK
STRANGER BY THE RIVER
COINS OF GOLD
ANITYA
ALL ABOUT ECK
THE KEY TO ECKANKAR
ECK AND MUSIC
WISDOM OF ECK
INTRODUCTION TO ECKANKAR